Three-Dimensional Art Adventures

First published in the United States of America in 2016
by Chicago Review Press Incorporated
814 North Franklin Street
Chicago, Illinois 60610
ISBN 978-1-61373-659-3

Conceived and produced by
Elwin Street Productions Limited
14 Clerkenwell Green
London EC1R 0DP
www.elwinstreet.com

The activities described in this book are to be carried out with parental supervision at all times. Every effort has been made to ensure the safety of the activities detailed. Neither the author nor the publishers shall be liable or responsible for any harm or damage done allegedly arising from any information or suggestion in this book.

Library of Congress Cataloging-In-Publication Data

Names: Pitamic, Maja, author. | Laidlaw, Jill A., author.
Title: Three-dimensional art adventures : 36 creative, artist-inspired
   projects in sculpture, ceramics, textiles, and more / Maja Pitamic and
   Jill Laidlaw.
Description: Chicago, Illinois : Chicago Review Press Incorporated, 2016. |
   Includes index.
Identifiers: LCCN 2015048885 | ISBN 9781613736593 (trade paper)
Subjects: LCSH: Sculpture—Juvenile literature. | Sculpture—Study and
   teaching (Elementary)—Activity programs.
Classification: LCC NB1143 .P58 2016 | DDC 730—dc23 LC record available at http://lccn.loc.gov/2015048885

Cover design: Rebecca Lown
Cover layout: Elwin Street Productions
Original photography: Ian Garlick

Printed in China
5 4 3 2 1

Three-Dimensional Art Adventures

36 Creative, Artist-Inspired Projects in
Sculpture, Ceramics, Textiles, and More

MAJA PITAMIC AND JILL LAIDLAW

CHICAGO
REVIEW
PRESS

Contents

Introduction

I like this book and I'm very pleased to recommend it. There are two simple reasons for this.

The first is that it will appeal to adults thinking about the development of children—whether your own, or groups in more formal education settings, or in art clubs. Children, of course, are the constant in all of these, but the role of interested and inspiring adults can't be underestimated.

I hope that the contents will encourage adults to experiment and enjoy playful activities together with those they had in mind when they bought the book. There are some delightful ideas here, which are clearly explained and well illustrated to aid a range of creative making. The variety of materials used or suggested will stretch the experiences of physical manipulation, as well as the intellectual and conceptualization processes, and probably spark many curious new investigations. All of which I not only heartily endorse but also can still find in my memories of similar projects from my own childhood! I should add that I'm still inspired by three-dimensional materials many decades later and spend much of my time encouraging teachers to be brave enough to explore them too.

My second reason is that this book allows children to encounter the works of many artists. The points of inspiration come from a range of places and time periods, and for me this is especially important. The notion of artists as dead, white European men is too often reinforced in the examples we choose to show children and young people. I'm really pleased to find examples here of global contemporary artists (both male and female), as well as artworks from ancient cultures where we have no idea of the identity of the artist. I think this is a very healthy reminder that the importance of making art is crucial to understanding human behavior, as well as the recognition that the creative drive is found in everyone.

Of course children may not fully understand the importance of these issues, but if we don't allow them to see or consider a wide range of artists it becomes quite easy to see how this carries restrictive and undesirable consequences.

I hope I've convinced every adult that thinks about the development of children and the educational (or wider learning) experiences that they want to share with or impart to youngsters to explore this book and the activities within it—and of course enjoy the making experience too.

Dr. Peter Gregory
Vice President, National Society of Education
in Art and Design (NSEAD)
Principal Lecturer in Education (Creative Arts),
Canterbury Christ Church University

How to use this book

Three-Dimensional Art Adventures introduces both adults and children to key works of three-dimensional art—which encompass a wealth of styles from ancient Greek sculpture to contemporary installations—and uses those works to inspire related art activities. You don't need to know anything about art history, because a short explanation of each sculpture, ceramic, textile, or installation is given along with the activities, as well as suggestions for how to explore the artworks further. The book is divided into periods and styles so you can easily observe developments through art history and understand how artists influence each other.

Most importantly, you don't even need to be able to draw, because all the projects are simple, easy to follow, and designed with children in mind. With *Three-Dimensional Art Adventures,* all you really need are youngsters with enthusiasm and creative, enquiring minds. Every activity contains a detailed materials list, clear step-by-step instructions paired with photographs, and top tips from the authors.

To enhance your adventures in art, you will find artists' biographies, a helpful glossary of art-related terms, and a list of locations where you can see the featured artworks in person at the back of the book. Furthermore our "Tools of the trade" page will give you some extra pointers that will help you make the most out of each activity.

This book evolves with your child; younger children might need assistance with the activities, but as they grow older they will be able to do the projects on their own. While all the activities are designed with children in mind, parents should always supervise when any sharp objects are required.

1 Early Sculpture

Nearly 1,500 years separate the two pieces of sculpture in this chapter. At first glance they might appear to have no connection—there are undeniable contrasts in scale, medium, and purpose—yet a common theme links the ancient bronze figure of a running girl to Donatello's *Annunciation*. Art from the period in which the bronze figure was made was regarded by Renaissance artists as the benchmark by which all sculpture should be judged, and Donatello studied classical sculpture in great depth. Strip away the decorative elements of the *Annunciation* and you discover the same purity of line that is found in the bronze figure. At their core, both pieces have an intimacy and humanity that transcend the years

Bronze Running Girl

Measuring only 4 inches (11 cm) tall this bronze figure of a running girl is one of the smallest pieces of sculpture that survives from the ancient world, and it holds a wealth of cultural and social significance.

Artist	Unknown
Nationality	Ancient Greek
Made	520–500 BCE

What's the story?

Our first clue as to the origins of this piece is a small rivet in the right foot, which suggests that the sculpture was once attached to another item, and the figure probably formed a decorative element on some vessel or utensil.

It was discovered in Prizren in Albania, but is in the Peloponnesian style and was created in what is now considered to be the golden age of Greek art.

Although described as a "running girl" the figure is probably an athlete, which suggests that the piece comes from the ancient Greek city-state of Sparta. It was only in Sparta that girls and women were allowed to compete as athletes. A sporting event, known as the "Heraia," was held every four years in honor of the goddess Hera. Pausanias (a Greek scholar and geographer who lived in the second century CE) describes the female athletes competing in these games in his *Periegesis Hellados* ("Description of Greece"): "Their hair hangs down, a tunic reaches to a little above the knee and they bare their right shoulder." This description matches the figure and the beautiful simplicity of line that effortlessly captures a sense of movement.

This sculpture is therefore special on two counts: first that it portrays a female athlete rather than a man, and second that it demonstrates how even the Spartans, with their fearsome warrior-like reputation, recognized the importance of the arts within their culture.

Think about . . .

What was the golden age of Greek art?
Greek arts flourished under the leadership of the Athenian general Pericles (495–429 BCE). Greek sculptors were interested in creating the ideal human form according to proportion, symmetry, and balance.

Who were the Spartans?
The ancient Greek city-state of Sparta was known for its powerful military strength, and all its citizens lived by a strict code of discipline and austerity. Yet creativity was also held in high regard, and boys joining the *agoge* (mandatory military training) would receive education in the arts as well.

"She isn't wearing any running shoes!"

Tom, age 7

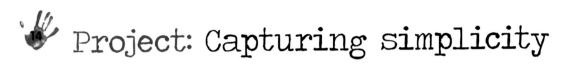

Project: Capturing simplicity

This project demonstrates the elegant simplicity of the original, but to make it easier to sculpt at home the figure is captured in silhouette, cut out in clay, and then painted bronze. We have used silver for the plinth and bronze for the figure, but you can experiment with any colors you like.

1 Make an outline drawing of the girl, roughly 6 x 6 inches (16 x 16 cm), on the cardboard; cut out and set aside. Then take your clay and divide it into three pieces: two large and one slighter smaller.

2 Take one of the larger pieces of clay. Roll it out evenly and cut into an 8 x 8 inch (20 x 20 cm) square. Set aside. Make the next piece into a 7 x 7 inch (18 x 18 cm) square, and the smallest piece of clay into a 6 x 6 inch (16 x 16 cm) square.

You will need

Piece of thin cardboard

Pencil

Wooden board or tray as work surface

Rolling pin

Ruler

Spray bottle filled with water

Plastic knife

Air-dry clay

Silver, gold, and bronze paint

Paintbrush

3 Use your template to cut out the girl from the smallest square. Then spray one side of the biggest square and the medium square with water. Score a crisscross pattern on the smaller square with the knife and press the two together.

4 Repeat the sticking process in step 3 to place the figure on top of the layers. Allow to dry, then paint and allow to dry again.

Top tips

• Smooth down the edges of the clay with your fingers between steps for a better finish.
• If your clay is drying out give it a quick spray with the water.
• The clay might take up to three days to dry completely, but you can speed up the process with a hair dryer.

Project: An impression of movement

One of the most striking things about the running girl sculpture is its sense of movement. Here we will make three sculptures, each in a different running position, to create a similar feeling of movement. You can make the figures as big or small as you want, but try not to think of them as three separate units. The figures come together as a harmonious whole and complement each other.

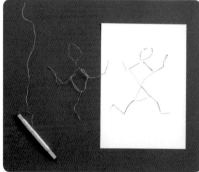

You will need

3 sheets of paper

Pencil

3 or more pieces of florist's wire

3 florist foam bases (you could use cork or a container filled with sand or plaster instead)

Spray paint (optional) for coloring bases

1 Make a simple line drawing of the figure on your paper. Repeat the drawing for a second and third time but with the figure in different positions. These drawings will act as your guides for your wire figures.

2 Fold a piece of wire in half; make a loop for the head and then the arms and legs to create a simple stick figure. Then shape the wire limbs to match your guide drawing.

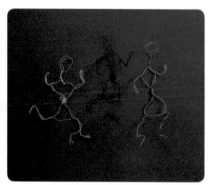

Top tips

• If using plaster as your base, allow it to set a little before inserting the figures, and make sure that your base is heavy enough to support them.
• You can choose to double the florist's wire for extra strength.

3 You can use one piece of wire, or add more details, such as feet and hair (remember to leave about 2 in/5 cm at the ends that will be buried in the base). Repeat these steps for the next two figures with differing positions for the arms and the legs to match your other two drawings.

4 Spread out the wire ends for the figures and set them into the bases. The figures may need some final adjustments to their shape. We have used spray paint to color the bases, but you can use any paint you have or simply leave them plain.

Annunciation Tabernacle

Donatello was a master of many art forms including sculpture and architecture. His art was widely celebrated, but just what was it about his work that his contemporaries so admired?

Artist	Donatello
Nationality	Italian
Made	around 1435

What's the story?

In his *Lives of the Artists* (1550), Giorgio Vasari says of Donatello: "His works showed so much grace, design and excellence, that they were held to approach the marvelous works of the ancient Greeks and Romans." This was the highest praise that could be awarded to a Renaissance artist, since the art of the Classical period was held in the highest regard at this time.

This *Annunciation* was commissioned by the Cavalcanti family for their chapel in the large Florentine church of Santa Croce. The Annunciation was a popular Renaissance subject that gave artists the opportunity to present a scene of dramatic contrasts. For Donatello, however, the drama is on a very human scale. The angel is portrayed not as a supernatural messenger but almost as an expected visitor gracefully kneeling before the Virgin. The figures form two sides of a graceful arc, while the eye contact between them conveys a sense of understanding and intimacy.

Within this richly decorated, shallow backdrop, Donatello presents a very private drama, to which we are onlookers. For Donatello, art is not only about creating a likeness of the human form, but also breathing life into the human drama embodied by them.

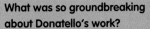
Think about . . .

What was so groundbreaking about Donatello's work?
Donatello and his architect friend Filippo Brunelleschi made close studies of the Greek and Roman ruins in Florence. Later, when Donatello was asked to create a statue of Saint George he made reference to the Greek bodily ideal by endowing the saint with perfect physical proportions. Nonetheless, the mental qualities of the saint are also revealed in his furrowed brow, which suggests an awareness of impending danger.

Donatello's work perfectly reflects the dramatic change in Renaissance art and society that saw Biblical themes and Christian values interpreted in a very human way.

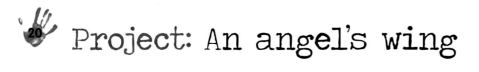

Project: An angel's wing

This project uses real feathers to create a mobile in the shape of an angel's wing. First we will paint the feathers in colors of your choice and then hang them to create the shape of the wing.

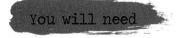

7 feathers

Fine paintbrush

Colored inks, poster paints, or food coloring

Scissors

Cotton thread

Needle

Metallic beads

1 stick, about 20 inches (50 cm) long

3 feet (1 m) of picture wire

Tape

1 Begin by painting your feathers. You can paint them any way you want, but allow them to dry before moving on to the next step.

2 Cut 7 pieces of thread, the first 28 inches (70 cm) long and then reduce each by 4 inches (10 cm) so the last is 4 inches (10 cm). Knot one piece at the end, then thread through one of the feathers and add some beads. Repeat with the other feathers.

3 Select the longest piece of thread and attach it with tape to the stick. Take the next longest thread and attach it next to the first feather. Repeat with the remaining threads and feathers.

4 Twist the ends of the wire around the stick to make a hanger in the shape of a triangle (secure with tape for extra strength if necessary). Your angel wing is now ready to display.

Top tips

• Experiment by spray painting the feathers or adding more beads.
• Try making another wing on the opposite diagonal to make a pair.
• Instead of a stick and wire you could just use wire, or try a coat hanger.

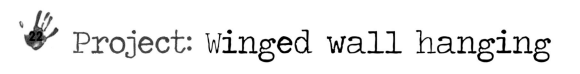

Project: Winged wall hanging

This wall hanging draws on elements from Donatello's *Annunciation* and uses them to create an abstract pattern. The design is inspired by the decorated spaces at the back of the relief, the feather print echoes the angel's wings, and the gold paint echoes the gilding of the original.

1 Cover your work area with newspaper. Stretch out your fabric and secure with tape so that it is taut. With gold and blue paint, practice some patterns on paper before trying them out on the fabric. Allow the paint to dry.

2 Cut the potato in half, lengthwise. Mark out a feather design in pencil on the potato flesh and ask an adult to help you carefully cut away the area outside the outline. Then add some finer details, such as the feather tips.

3 Cover the potato "feather" with black paint. Practice printing it on a piece of paper before printing on the fabric. You can print the feather in a pattern or randomly. Allow to dry.

4 Attach the top edge of your fabric to the stick with tape, then wrap the ends of your wire around the stick to create a hanger.

Top tips

• Any paint will do, but a metallic fabric paint gives a lovely effect.
• You can also try making the colors run a little by applying a spritz of water with a spray bottle.
• Always be very careful when using a sharp knife. Ask an adult to help you.

2 Modern Sculpture

In the past sculptures were often created as
monuments intended to celebrate or commemorate
someone or something—such as a great battle or
a political leader. Modern sculpture, however, often
makes a personal statement by the artist, using
materials undreamed of by sculptors of the past, such
as plastics, steel, iron, and fiberglass. In this chapter
we look at Louise Bourgeois's towering spider, with
its sense of a mother's protectiveness; the gigantic
proportions of Claes Oldenburg's *Trowel*; Umberto
Boccioni's *Unique Forms of Continuity in Space*; and the
dreamlike *Tulips of Shangri-La* by Yayoi Kusama.

Maman

For a lot of people, just the thought of a spider makes them anxious, so standing under a model of a spider more than 30 feet (9 m) tall would be their worst possible nightmare. Yet this spider sculpture standing in the entrance of the Tate Modern's massive turbine hall proved to be a great draw, and artist Louise Bourgeois went on to produce several more, which have been displayed in art galleries across the world.

Artist	Louise Bourgeois
Nationality	French American
Made	1999

What's the story?

Bourgeois's work covers many decades, during which time she was always aware of developing art movements, but she was always an innovator, never a follower. She explores her art through varied media of painting, print-making, sculpture, installation, and performance and uses innovative materials including wood, steel, rubber, and fabric.

The spider sculptures were, for Bourgeois, the culmination of a long career that embodied realism, drawing upon sometimes painful memories of her childhood for their subject matter. But in all this exploration Bourgeois has always strived to create her own style, never afraid to expose her truth, however uncomfortable that may be, and she challenges us to do the same. The spider is her final tribute to her mother.

The clue is in the title *Maman*, which means "mother" in French. "The spider is an ode to my mother. She was my best friend. Like a spider my mother was a weaver. Like spiders my mother was very clever. Spiders are friendly presences that eat mosquitoes. So spiders are helpful and protective, just like my mother."

Why did Bourgeois choose a spider as the subject, which many people would see as scary?
Bourgeois sees spiders differently than other people do, and this comes across in her sculpture. This spider has been created as a protective presence, with legs resembling needles, protecting her marble eggs in a mesh sac, ever watchful and wakeful. Imagine this sculpture without those things and perhaps you will find it produces a very different feeling.

If you were to make a sculpture of a family member in the form of an animal, what animal would you choose and why? Think about the scale, material, and color.

Project: Model spider

Louise Bourgeois used a mixture of natural and man-made materials to create her spider sculpture, so this spider model also uses mixed materials: modeling clay for the body and pipe cleaners for the legs. Pipe cleaners are highly flexible, making them ideal for bending into different leg shapes, and their fabric covering suggests the hairy nature of a spider's legs.

1 Divide the large clay ball into two halves. Roll one half into a ball; this will form the main part of the spider's body.

2 Take the other ball and divide it in half again. Roll one half into a long, thin sausage shape, and then shape it into an upward spiral. With the remaining half, roll out several small strips that will form the egg sac.

You will need

Ball of modeling clay about the size of a tennis ball

Smaller ball of modeling clay in a contrasting color

8 pipe cleaners in any color or two contrasting colors

3 Use the clay in the contrasting color to make several small balls that will become the eggs.

4 Slightly flatten one end of the body ball and place the eggs on top. Now take the strips and place them over the eggs in a crisscross fashion, working the clay together with your fingers.

Top tips

• You don't have to make your spider the same size as the one here. It could be larger or smaller, or you could even make a whole family. Just make sure that the body and legs are in proportion to each other so that it will stand up on its own.

• This spider is black to match the original sculpture, but you can experiment with other colors for the clay and the pipe cleaners.

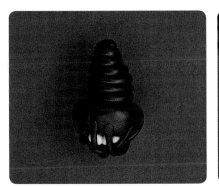

5 Place the spiral of clay on the other end of the body ball, again working in the edges with your fingers to join the two.

6 Insert four pipe cleaners on each side of the body. Bend and position them to give the impression of the spider in movement.

Project: Woven web

A web forms the perfect background to your spider model, and as a reminder that a spider is a weaver, like Louise Bourgeois's mother, this web is made from yarn. You can use any colors you like, either to complement or contrast with your spider model.

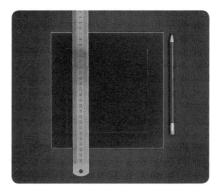

1 Mark out a rectangle on the cardboard, leaving a frame of about 1 inch (3 cm). Cut out the rectangle. If the cardboard is extra thick, you may need an adult to help you with this.

2 Use the hole punch to make a hole in each of the corners, the horizontal edges, and the vertical edges, making a total of eight holes. Again, you may need the help of an adult.

You will need

Sheet of 8 ½ x 14-inch (Legal) cardboard

Pencil

Ruler

Scissors

Single-hole punch, or something to make holes

Two balls of yarn in different colors

Large plastic needle

Clear glue

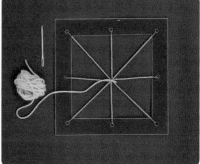

4 Continue looping the yarn through the holes so that you end up with the yarn stretched out between the corners and edges, like the spokes of a wheel. Cut off the end of the yarn and tie the two loose ends in a knot to secure.

5 With the other color of yarn, roughly measure out the amount you will need by making a spiral pattern on top of the strung yarn, and double it to allow extra for the weaving and threading of the needle.

3 Thread the yarn through the needle. Insert it through one corner hole, then continue to the opposite corner so the yarn stretches diagonally across. Loop back through one of the adjacent holes, then straight down to the opposite hole again.

6 Thread the needle. Loop through the center and knot to secure. Now weave through the threads in a spiral pattern, looping around each spoke to hold it in place. When you reach the frame, tie the end to one of the lengths of yarn at the back of the frame to secure.

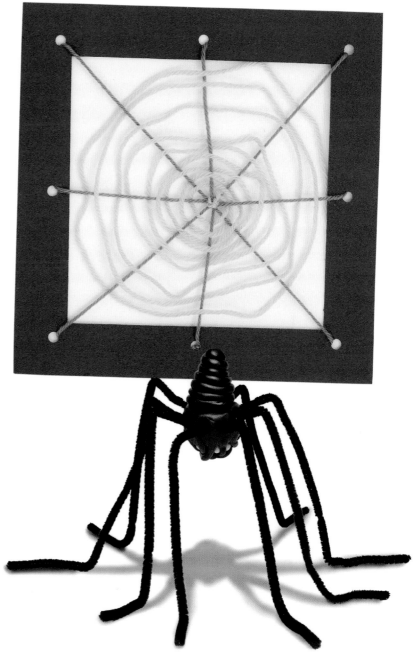

Trowel

Claes Oldenburg turns sculpture on its head with his sculpture *Trowel*; the ordinary becomes the extraordinary as we are asked to reconsider an everyday object in a new light. There is drama through the use of scale and color, and humor in the way the subject is viewed. The use of everyday objects as subjects for his work closely linked him with the Pop Art movement of the 1960s.

Artist	Claes Oldenburg
Nationality	American
Made	2001

What's the story?

"My single-minded aim is to give existence to fantasy," Claes Oldenburg has said about his work. With this piece, Oldenburg gives free rein to his fantasy. The appeal of the sculpture lies partly in its monumental scale—nearly 25 feet (7.5 m) in height. It is as if a giant has playfully thrust his trowel into the earth.

The simplicity of the design, with its continuous flowing curves, gives the whole structure a sense of movement and creates a relation between the shapes. Oldenburg cleverly uses the natural outside setting of the Serralves Museum of contemporary art in Portugal to add extra drama using the surrounding natural colors and light. The different materials used, including steel, aluminum, and fiber-reinforced plastic, along with polyurethane enamel paint, combine to make lots of light-reflective surfaces.

This *Trowel* is one of several sculptures that Oldenburg made for commissions in public spaces. His lighthearted approach shows in his other works as well, from huge popsicles made from furry fabrics to a giant flashlight that switches on and off.

Think about . . .

What effect is produced by the trowel's gigantic scale?
Initially one of surprise at its size, and then amusement that such a common object should be the subject of a giant sculpture. In the past, sculptures of this scale would have been constructions of a serious nature, commemorating notable people and events.

Why does this sculpture have more impact outside than it would in a gallery?
Oldenburg makes good use of the natural surroundings: the red of the corrugated metal sings out against the background of the green trees and bushes. It is offset by the brilliant sunshine under the azure blue of a clear sky, the effect of which will change according to the time of day.

Project: Nuts-and-bolts sculpture

It would be difficult to make something on the same massive scale as Oldenburg's *Trowel*, but in this project you can explore the dynamic effect that using different shapes and bright colors can have on a sculpture.

1 Use a damp sponge or brush to paint one of the pieces of construction paper three-quarters blue and one-quarter green. Set aside to dry. Repeat this step on your other sheet using your choice of colors.

4 Now let your imagination run wild: embed your nuts, bolts, and wall plugs into the clay any way you like. Set aside.

2 Put your rice into the bowl, add a few drops of the food coloring, and mix so that the color is evenly distributed and then set aside.

3 Model your clay into a tower with a wide base tapering into a narrower shape at the top. Make sure that it can stand upright.

Sponge or paintbrush

Two 8 ½ x 14-inch (Legal) sheets of construction paper

Blue and green watercolor paints, plus two more colors

Raw rice, enough to cover the shallow circular dish

Pink food coloring

Bowl and spoon for mixing

Shallow circular dish, about 11 inches (30 cm) in diameter

Piece of modeling clay, enough to make a tower shape roughly 1 x 10 inches (3 x 25 cm)

Small selection of nuts and bolts

6–10 red wall plugs

Poster tack

Spoon

5 Put small pieces of poster tack along the longer edge of your blue-and-green paper and stick it around one side of the circular dish. It should cover roughly half the circumference and will form the backdrop to your sculpture.

6 Spread the rice evenly in the shallow dish and leave a space big enough for your sculpture. Once in place, cover the base of your sculpture with the rice. Your sculpture is now ready to show off! Change the backdrop to see how it alters the look of your piece.

Top tip

Make sure you don't allow the clay to dry out, or you won't be able to embed your nuts and bolts.

Project: Reflection sculpture

In this project we will discover how using elements of light and water can produce an even bigger impact on the dynamic of a work, adding extra dimensions to your sculpture.

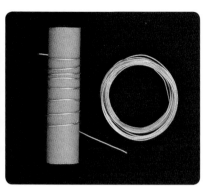

1 Spiral the wire around the tube. Once you have the basic shape, remove the tube and continue weaving the wire vertically, in and out of the tower shape, ensuring that the tower is able to stand upright.

2 Cut your cellophane into small strips and weave these through the wire tower.

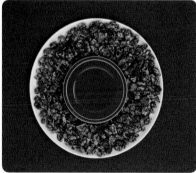

3 Measure and cut a piece of foil big enough to cover the paper, allowing an extra ½ inch (1 cm) all around. Position the paper in the center of the foil. Fold over the edges and stick down with tape. Also stick pieces of the tape along one of the longer edges on the front of the foil-covered surface.

4 Place your dish in the center of the tray and place the pebbles in the remaining tray space. Place your wire tower in the center of the dish and fill with water to just below the edge of the dish. Stick the foil card around the edge of the tray, to form the backdrop to your sculpture.

You will need

Small tube or container, roughly 1 ½ x 8 inches (4 x 20 cm)

Enough modeling or gardener's wire to wrap around the whole tube, plus a little extra

Colored cellophane, red and blue (candy wrappers also work well)

Scissors

Sheet of 8 ½ x 11-inch (Letter) paper

Aluminum foil

Double-sided tape

Shallow circular dish, about 6 inches (15 cm) in diameter

Shallow tray, preferably circular, about 11 inches (30 cm) in diameter

Assortment of pebbles and stones

Top tip

Place your sculpture in a sunny position —for example, on a windowsill—to take full advantage of light's changing effects.

Unique Forms of Continuity in Space

Umberto Boccioni was one of the most prominent artists of the Futurist art movement, and produced the *Technical Manifesto of Futurist Sculpture* in 1912. His work could be said to be a complete break with the past and represents a fitting interpretation of "Modern," perfectly encapsulating the Futurist ideals, which held modern technology as the ultimate pinnacle of human achievement, one that would create a new world. In art form, these ideas were expressed through dynamism and speed.

Artist	Umberto Boccioni
Nationality	Italian
Made	1913

What's the story?

During 1911 and 1912, Boccioni developed an interest in both Cubism and sculpture, and we see the combination of these two movements in his famous sculpture *Unique Forms of Continuity in Space*.

It is unclear whether the resplendent figure is supposed to depict a man or a woman, because the face is devoid of features. He or she appears more like a superhero striding toward the future with full force. The feeling of dynamic movement is achieved by the very organic shapes; there are no straight lines—one form feeds into another.

The sculpture as a plaster cast was found in his studio, after his untimely death in 1916, during World War I, and it was recast in bronze in 1949. While the Futurists vision of a "New World" was laid bare by World War I, Boccioni's Futurist *Manifesto* on sculpture was to lay the foundation for sculptors in the following generations. He proclaimed in 1912: "These days I am obsessed by sculpture! I believe I have glimpsed a complete renovation of that mummified art."

Think about

In what way could Boccioni's sculpture be seen as a complete break with the past?
Boccioni captures the mood of the moment, in which young artists were striving to break with the artists of the past. Technology was to be the way forward, and this idea is shown as dynamic movement, motion, and speed—the figure is captured midstride, and the curvy lines and shapes suggest that sense of constant movement.

Why do you think Boccioni makes the figure's facial features so unidentifiable?
"Blurred" features give the impression of movement, just like a photograph taken in motion.

Project: Superhero sculpture

This project attempts to capture the energy and motion of Boccioni's sculpture by using clay to create dynamic forms and a sense of movement.

1 Use the wire to form the basic structure of your figure. To make sure the figure can stand upright, anchor the feet of your wire sculpture in a little clay on a plastic container lid.

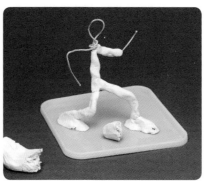

2 Knead the clay until smooth. Break off sections and model it around the wire figure. Build up each section so that the body parts are in proportion to each other.

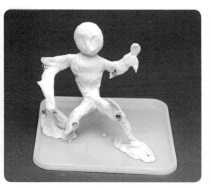

3 Pinch the clay to create indents and shapes in the figure. Try to create the effect of flags blowing in the wind—like the fabric blowing back around the figure's legs in Boccioni's sculpture. Let dry.

4 Paint your figure in your choice of metallic color. Allow it to dry and then insert the brads into the figure's "joints."

You will need

Wire, to form a structure for your figure

Modeling clay, enough to cover a figure about 8 inches (20 cm) high

Plastic container lid or tray

Brads

Double-sided tape or glue

Enough bronze, gold, or silver paint to cover your figure

Large paintbrush

Top tips

• Don't show any clear features on the face—it should look masklike.
• If you can't find bronze paint, you can add a little brown paint to gold to create the same effect.

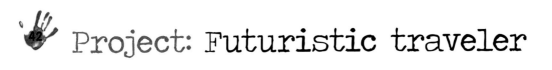

Project: Futuristic traveler

Boccioni's figure looks like it could be from the future or stepping out of a science fiction movie, so in this activity we will make a space traveler striding through the universe. We can borrow a device used by the Futurists to suggest movement and motion by repeating the figure and smudging the paint to give a blurred effect.

You will need

Dark blue, light blue, gold, sliver, and white acrylic or poster paint

Paintbrush

Canvas or thick cardboard

Fine-tipped pen

Piece of 8 ½ x 11-inch (Letter) thin cardboard

2 paper or plastic plates

Scissors

Water to clean your brushes

1 Cover the whole surface of your canvas or thick cardboard with the light blue paint. Allow to dry.

2 Draw the outline of Boccioni's figure on the thin cardboard and cut out. Place the template on the left side of the canvas and trace around it. Move along and draw around it again. Repeat in a wave pattern until you reach the right side.

3 Pour out some gold and silver paint. Dip your finger in the gold paint and dot all over the first figure. Repeat this step filling in the gaps with the silver paint. Blend the colors loosely together to fill in any gaps. Now do the same for the other figures.

4 When the gold and silver paint have dried use the black paint to shadow the front of the figures. Then add some dark blue shades to the sky. Then dip your finger into some white paint and dot over the blue pattern to represent stars.

Top tip

You will need to work quickly when applying the gold and silver paint because it needs to still be wet when smudging it.

The Tulips of Shangri-La

Yayoi Kusama is one of the world's most popular living artists. In a career that has embraced all types of media, including painting, drawing, sculpture, film, performance, installation, and fashion, she has created a completely distinctive style.

Artist	Yayoi Kusama
Nationality	Japanese
Made	2003

What's the story?

In the 1960s, Kusama moved from her native Japan to the "happening" art scene of New York, where she was given the name "Polka-dot princess" by the paparazzi.

Shangri-La is an imaginary, exotic, perfect land, and this sculpture, *The Tulips of Shangri-La*, is one of a series known as *The Flowers That Bloom at Midnight*. In it we see a combination of her two loves, polka dots and flowers, both of which are recurring elements in her work.

This sculpture was made for a public space at the railroad station in Lille, France. It is made from fiberglass and reinforced plastic, and then painted by hand. The giant flowers, measuring 5–10 feet (1.5–3.5 m), take on a surreal (strange) form a bit like the imagined landscapes of *Alice in Wonderland*. The flamboyant colors, dramatic pattern, and sensuous forms conjure up a kind of Shangri-La.

In the 1970s Kusama returned to Japan, continuing to explore and develop her style. While her work may at times appear whimsical and humorous, like Louise Bourgeois's, she is fearless in her quest for her art, creating works that are "celebrations of potential vulnerability and defiance."

Think about . . .

Why do you think Kusama chooses to decorate this sculpture and many other of her works with polka dots? For Kusama the dots are an expression of who she is and how she fits into the wider world; you may like to take a look at some of her other "dot" works such as *Ascension of the Polkadots on Trees*, *Dots Obsession*, and *Red Pumpkin*.

If you had to choose a color or a pattern to represent you, what would you choose and why?

"These flowers are very bright and colorful."
Susie, age 8

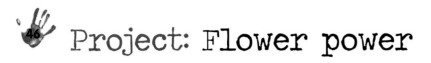

Project: Flower power

This art activity sets out to capture the playful, surreal nature of *The Tulips of Shangri-La*. The flowers and their pot are decorated with tissue paper and paint, so use your imagination and get creative when it comes to choosing colors and patterns!

1 Paint the pot in the colors and patterns of your choice. Set aside and allow it to dry.

4 Repeat step 3 until you have three or four flowers. Cut 4-inch (10 cm) lengths of the pipe cleaners, two per flower. Loop these through the gaps between two petals. Pull the ends together and curl the ends to form stamen.

You will need

Small terra-cotta pot

Poster or acrylic paint in bright colors, including white

Paintbrush

Florist's foam

Sharp knife

Scissors

Roll of garden wire

4–5 pipe cleaners

Selection of colored tissue paper

Glue stick

Dark felt-tip pen

Green scouring pad

2 Shape the florist's foam to fit inside the terra-cotta pot (you may need an adult to help with this).

3 Cut a piece of wire about 28 inches (70 cm) long. About 6 inches (15 cm) from one end, loop the wire into a petal, and repeat to form five petals, shaping them so that the first and last loops are next to each other. Twist the remaining straight lengths of wire together to form a stem.

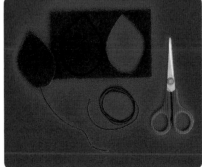

5 Cut pieces of colored tissue to cover the petals. Brush glue onto the wire of your petals and wrap the tissue around. Add at least two layers per petal. Set aside to dry.

6 With the felt-tip pen, draw some leaves on the green scouring pad and cut them out. Run a length of wire through each leaf and attach the other end to a flower stem. Arrange your flowers in the pot, pushing the ends of the stems into the foam.

Top tips

• Your flowers can be any size, but remember to make them in scale with their container.
• You could try this project using different materials such as cellophane or wrapping paper.

Project: Bees and butterflies

Continuing the surrealist humor, try adding some larger-than-life bees and butterflies to your quirky flower display.

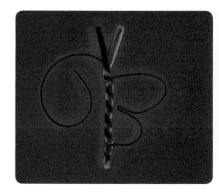

1 To make the butterfly body, twist together the pipe cleaners, leaving about 1 inch (3 cm) untwisted. Cut 20 inches (50 cm) of wire and bend into the shape of wings. Wrap them around the body at top and bottom.

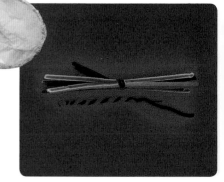

4 To make the bee, twist together a yellow and a black pipe cleaner around a length of garden wire about 8 inches (20 cm) long. Leave about 1 inch (3 cm) untwisted.

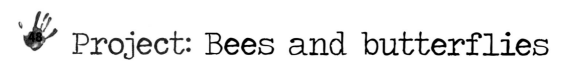

49

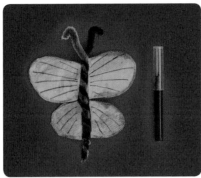

2 Tear up pieces of tissue paper to add to your wings. Apply glue to the wire frame, and wrap the tissue around each section, adding at least two layers to each.

3 Allow to dry, then add any details you like to your wings; for example, add wing scale details using a fine felt-tip pen. Or you could add other patterns or colors. Curl up the untwisted pipe cleaner ends into antennae.

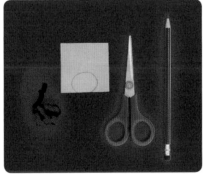

5 Wrap the body around a thin cylindrical object, like a pen or a paintbrush, to coil it into a spring shape. Remove the bee body and push the loops of spiral together. The untwisted ends are the bee's antennae.

6 Use a pencil to trace some wings onto tissue paper. Cut them out and stick them on the bee body. Attach lengths of wire to both your butterfly and your bee, and insert them into the florist's foam.

Top tips

• You could add different insects, such as ladybugs or caterpillars.
• When using the felt tip on the tissue paper, press very lightly to avoid tearing the tissue.

3 Installation

Installation art can be made of anything—from video recordings to sound, light, metal, plastic, or stone. Installation art is sometimes made for a place outdoors but is also often found in specific spaces within art galleries. Installation art can be permanent or temporary (only supposed to exist for a short period of time). When you see a painting or a sculpture, you can look at it; but with an installation you can see it, touch it, hear it, or walk through it. In this chapter Ai Weiwei's *Forever Bicycles* uses an everyday object to make us think about how things change over time, Alex Chinneck's *From the Knees of My Nose to the Belly of My Toes* makes us smile, and Rachel Whiteread's *Embankment* shows us how a whole landscape can be made out of boxes.

Forever Bicycles

This open-air installation in Venice, Italy, is made of 1,179 bicycles. Every single one of the bicycles is the same color and size so that when they are all put together they look like one huge pattern made out of metal.

Artist	Ai Weiwei
Nationality	Chinese
Made	2014

What's the story?

Bicycles used to be the most common kind of transport in China—the country was often called the world capital of bicycles, and it manufactured more than a million of them every year. When Ai Weiwei, the artist who made *Forever Bicycles*, was a child the most popular brand of bicycle was the "Forever Bicycle," and if you knew someone who owned this type of bike, you thought that they were very lucky because you wanted a Forever Bicycle too. *Forever Bicycles* is made out of only one kind of bike—the Forever Bicycle.

China has since become a much richer country and people don't want to use bicycles to get around anymore—they want to own cars. Ai Weiwei thinks that this switch from using bicycles to using cars shows how much China has changed, and he's a little sad that bicycles are being thrown away and cars are taking their place; bicycles are good for exercise, but cars pollute the air and this is now a big problem in Chinese cities.

By sticking all of the bicycles in *Forever Bicycles* together Ai Weiwei has made them useless—you can't play on them, and they can't take you anywhere. So maybe bicycles are not forever . . .

How does *Forever Bicycles* work as an installation?
Ai Weiwei has arranged the bicycles so that there are tunnels that worm their way through the bicycles at ground level, so people can walk through the them, from one side to the other. When you walk through the bicycles you can see them from unusual angles.

Are there still lots of bicycles in China?
Twenty years ago there were 670 million bicycles in China, but now there are only 430 million bicycles. More and more people in China can afford cars; in 2014 China bought a quarter of all the cars produced in the world.

"All those bikes together look like a climbing frame."
Molly, age 8

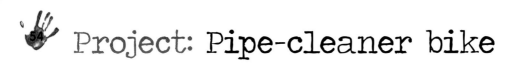

Project: Pipe-cleaner bike

Make a bicycle out of pipe cleaners and buttons, then use it as
a badge by attaching it to your clothes with two safety pins.
You could also use this bicycle as a three-dimensional part of a
picture by drawing a landscape and gluing the bike onto it.

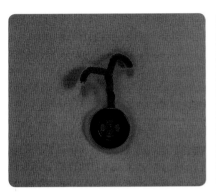

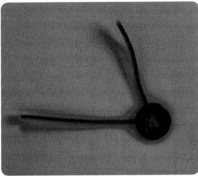

1 Thread a pipe cleaner through two of the holes of one of the buttons. Twist the two strands of the pipe cleaner around each other and make the shape of the bike's handlebars.

2 Thread the second pipe cleaner through the other button. This time push the pipe cleaner through all four holes, ending up with both ends behind the front of the button.

Top tips

• Choose buttons that have large holes in the middle—it will make it easier to push the pipe cleaners through.
• Try making a pipe-cleaner person to sit on your bike.

3 On the second button, twist one end of the pipe cleaner to become the bike's seat. Take the other end of the pipe cleaner and thread it behind the first button and through two holes on this button. Bend the end behind the first button wheel to secure it.

4 Take the third pipe cleaner and twist it around the bottom of the Y of the handlebars. Link the other end of the pipe cleaner to the back of the second wheel of the bike. Twist this pipe cleaner up to the seat. This will make your bike much stronger.

Project: String sculptures

Ai Weiwei can take everyday objects and make them into an installation. When you look at *Forever Bicycles* close up it looks like a tangle of lines. In this project you can turn leftover pieces of string into your own tangled sculpture.

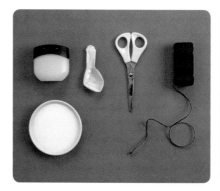

1 This project can be very messy, so put on some old clothes or wear an apron. Make sure your work surface is very well covered with newspaper and set out your materials. Pour a good amount of glue into a shallow dish and set aside.

2 Blow up your balloon—the larger the balloon the more string you will need, so start small if this is a first attempt. Cover the balloon in a thin layer of petroleum jelly and also add some to the rim of your cup.

Newspaper

Glue

Shallow dish

Ball of colored string

Petroleum jelly

Balloon

Cup

3 Cut a long length of string and dip it in your glue so it is well covered. This can be very messy! Tie the end of the string around the knot in the balloon and begin winding it around. Keep doing this until you have wrapped as much string as you want.

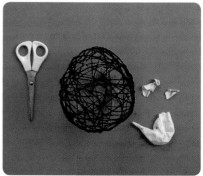

4 Sit the balloon on top of the cup. If any bits of string stick out then put a bit more glue on with your fingers and press them down. Leave the balloon on the cup to dry. When the string is dry and hard, pop the balloon and remove it from your sculpture.

Top tips

• The thinner the string you use, the quicker it will dry (it might take a day or two).

• We used colored string, but you can use plain and add food coloring to the glue.

• Try making lots of string sculptures in different colors.

From the Knees of My Nose to the Belly of My Toes

The front of this building is no longer standing upright, but its windows are not smashed and its bricks are not broken. This house has not fallen down; it has slipped down so that part of it rests on the ground. How is this possible?

Artist	Alex Chinneck
Nationality	British
Made	2013

What's the story?

London-based artist Alex Chinneck chose a house in Margate (an English seaside town) that had been empty for eleven years and decided to make it into a work of art. Chinneck says that he wants to make artworks that "astound people and cheer them up a bit."

Chinneck had $150,000 to spend on his project, but converting the house into an artwork was so expensive that he had to ask local construction companies to give him building materials for nothing; lots of workmen also helped by giving their time and skills for free. Even with the help of ten construction companies, *From the Knees of My Nose to the Belly of My Toes* took six months to complete.

The biggest part of Chinneck's plan involved taking the front of the house off and then building a new one that sloped to the ground. The new housefront had to have specially made window frames, glass, and a door that were curved in exactly the right places so that they could stretch between the part of the house that was still upright and the part of the house that bent down to lie flat on the ground.

Think about...

Does anyone live in this house?
If you look at the top of the house you can see an attic that is dirty and messy, but attics are usually run-down, unlived-in spaces so this doesn't give us any clues. The rest of the house looks clean, with new curtains in the windows and a satellite dish on the wall; the artist is playing another joke on us by trying to make us believe that the house is still being lived in.

What does the title of this artwork mean?
Try to put your nose on your knees. Now try to put your tummy on your toes. You can probably put your nose on your knees but not your tummy on your toes—it's impossible, just like the front of this house!

"It looks
like that
house has
melted."
Andrew, age 10

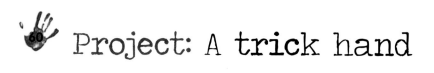

Project: A trick hand

Alex Chinneck's art plays tricks on you when you look at it. This project shows you how to play a trick of your own and draw a hand as if it is coming out of a sheet of paper. This effect is called an optical illusion.

1 Take a sheet of paper and put one of your hands flat on it. Draw around your hand using the pencil.

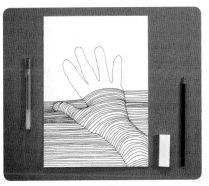

2 Fill in the background by drawing straight lines with a fine-tip pen. You don't need to use a ruler to draw these lines if you don't want to. Do not draw any straight lines inside the hand outline.

You will need

Plain white paper, any size you want to use

Pencil

Fine black pen

Ruler

Eraser

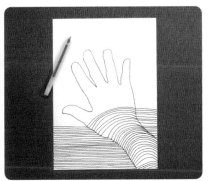

3 Start to draw lines inside the hand outline—but make these lines curved, like small hills—and connect the curved lines to the straight lines.

Top tips

• Try drawing different three-dimensional objects.
• Try using pens of different thicknesses and colors to get different effects.
• If you draw the lines closer together, the object looks "steeper" at that point.
• Make a frame for your picture from colored card or paper.

4 Gradually move up, filling the sheet with straight and curved lines. When you have filled in the whole thing use the eraser to rub out the original pencil outline.

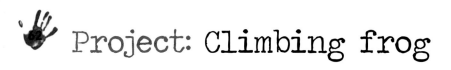

Project: Climbing frog

Another optical illusion that you can try is this simple drawing trick. By using the lines on a ruled piece of paper you can make a frog appear as if it is clinging onto some of the lines and climbing through the page. You can also try this trick with any animal you like.

Sheet of lined paper, any size

Pencil

Ruler

Fine black pen

Eraser

Colored pencils

1 Use the ruler and the pencil to draw along two of the lines on your paper. Now draw four sets of frog feet onto and around these lines. You don't have to draw in too much detail.

2 Draw over the frog's feet with a black pen. Take extra care not to draw over the two vertical pencil lines in black pen.

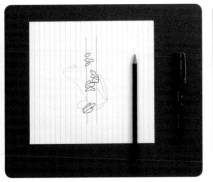

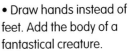

Top tips

• Draw hands instead of feet. Add the body of a fantastical creature.
• Turn your sheet on its side and draw hands hanging onto an imaginary pole created by a line of the paper. Now draw a person dangling by his or her hands from the pole.
• Make a frame for your picture from colored card or paper.

3 Draw the frog's body in pencil.

4 Go over your frog drawing in black pen. Then rub out the remaining pencil lines. Now color your frog in. Adding more detail when you color it in will make the illusion even more realistic.

Embankment

Rachel Whiteread created *Embankment* out of 14,000 boxes made of white plastic that you can almost—but not quite—see through. The boxes are the sizes and shapes of boxes you see every day, such as storage boxes, shoe boxes, and cardboard boxes.

Artist	Rachel Whiteread
Nationality	British
Made	2005

What's the story?

Embankment was made for the Turbine Hall, a huge space at the center of the Tate Modern art gallery in London. Whiteread piled the boxes she made into cubes and stacks. Seen altogether these shapes look like a landscape inside the hall. Whiteread even made some of the boxes topple over to make this landscape look more natural, as if it were changing in the way that mountains or buildings change over time. When you walk through the hall, you walk through a landscape the artist has created.

Whiteread came up with the idea for *Embankment* when she was going through her mother's belongings after she died and she found some of her things stored in a worn-out cardboard box; this started Whiteread thinking about the things we put in boxes. Soon after the artist began to notice boxes everywhere: empty or broken boxes lying in the street or boxes used to store toys or junk. Even though the boxes in *Embankment* are empty, the artist is asking us to imagine what could be in them —to think about all the special memories, secrets, and precious objects that belong to each of us.

Think about . . .

Why is this installation called *Embankment*?
The Tate Modern is on the bank of the river Thames in London, United Kingdom. A riverbank is called an embankment. So this installation's title is not only about where the artwork could be found but also about the installation itself—the boxes are piled so high that they become embankments, or steep barriers, themselves.

How long did it take to make *Embankment*?
It took five weeks to fill the space with Whiteread's boxes.

What happened to all the boxes?
After the installation was taken down the boxes were recycled.

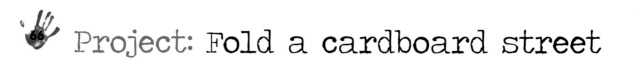

Project: Fold a cardboard street

Rachel Whiteread was inspired by everyday cardboard boxes to create a whole landscape that tells a complex story. This project shows you how to use cardboard to make your own street of individual houses. You can make as many or as few as you like, and you can even decorate them like real houses.

1 Cut the thin cardboard to 8 inches (20 cm) long by 2 inches (5 cm) wide. Using the ruler measure 2 inches (5 cm) along the strip and mark with a line. This is a "wall." Now measure 1½ inches (4 cm) for the floor and another 2 inches (5 cm) for the opposite wall.

2 Now mark 1 inch (2.5 cm) and another 1 inch (2.5 cm) for the roof. Lastly, mark another ½ inch (1 cm) and fold the card at the lines you have marked. Then turn the card over and decorate your house with pictures of doors, windows, or tiles.

3 Put some glue on the ½ inch (1 cm) tab and stick the house together. Make as many houses as you want and vary the sizes, but remember to keep the roof and wall lengths even or you will get a crooked house!

4 Finally, arrange pictures of outdoor images on the thicker cardboard to make a background for your street and then glue them in place. Then arrange your houses in front of it to complete your scene.

Top tips

• Experiment with other sizes; try doubling the lengths to make a house twice as big.
• You can leave the houses plain or decorate them in pen and add extra details.

Project: Craft storage box

Rachel Whiteread thought a lot about boxes and the things we might keep in them. This project shows you how to use boxes within boxes to create a tidy storage space for your arts and craft supplies. An organizer like this makes it easier to pack lots and lots of things into a small space.

1 Try fitting the small tubes and boxes inside the larger box. When you find a pattern you like make a quick sketch so that you don't forget.

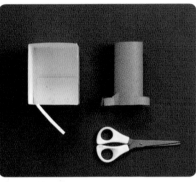

2 If any of the boxes or tubes stick out of the storage box because they are too tall, cut them down to fit.

You will need

Cardboard box or shoe box

Small cardboard boxes and tubes of different shapes and sizes that fit inside the bigger box

Pencil and scrap paper

Scissors

Poster paint

Paintbrush

Glue

Top tip

You can put anything in your storage box, for example a collection of shells and stones, or your favorite toy cars.

3 Paint your storage box any color you want. Then paint the small tubes and boxes that will become the compartments. You can leave some of them unpainted if you want to.

4 When everything is dry, glue the compartments inside the box using your plan as a guide and let dry. Then fill your storage box with craft supplies, such as pencils, pens, string, chalk, erasers, and paints.

4 Ceramics

The ceramic pieces in this chapter are striking in
their contrasts. They demonstrate the diversity
of the medium and prove that ceramics should be
as highly regarded as painting or sculpture. Each
of the artists in this chapter were drawn to ceramics
for very personal reasons. Bernard Palissy saw ceramics
as a way to give form to his philosophy of the natural
world. For Picasso, ceramics represented a release
from the intensity of painting; he enjoyed the sensual
nature of the medium, which matched his own earthy
personality. And while Leoncillo's ceramics outwardly
represent musical instruments, they also demonstrate
how music can represent feelings.

Dish with a Snake

The creatures depicted in *Dish with a Snake* are so naturalistic that it would seem a shame to cover them up with food. So could this extraordinary dish have been created for another reason?

Artist	Bernard Palissy
Nationality	French
Made	16th century

What's the story?

The dish comes from the studio of Bernard Palissy, an eccentric French potter whose work was so popular during his lifetime that he was awarded the special title of Inventeur des Rustiques du Roy (King's inventor of Rustic Ceramics) by King Henry II of France and his queen, Catherine de Médicis.

This title also demonstrates how, at that time, the decorative arts (which included ceramics) were very highly valued and could command as high a price as any painting or sculpture.

Palissy's ceramic creations were a reflection of his fascination with nature. The stunning realism of the snake and other creatures on this dish is no accident, but the result of endless hours of research. Like Leonardo da Vinci before him, Palissy's knowledge was based on experience, and he spent many years studying, sketching, and sculpting different animals. He even wrote two books on the subject.

An amazing sense of movement and energy is captured here: the frog seems about to spring off the dish, the fish appear to be swimming away, and you can almost hear the hiss of the slithering snake.

Think about . . .

What does *rustic* mean?
Rustic can mean of the country, homespun, or unsophisticated. In the French court of Versailles it was fashionable to dress up as shepherds and shepherdesses to create a rustic ideal. Also the 16th century saw the first imports of smooth porcelain from China, and the "rustic" earthenware that the snake dish is made from has a much coarser finish than the new porcelain.

Who was the dish made for and why?
Quite often elaborate dishes like these were made for a special occasion like a marriage, or it could have been made for a family or company with marine interests. There are dishes similar to this one around the world.

"The fish look like they are swimming on the plate."
Katie, age 7

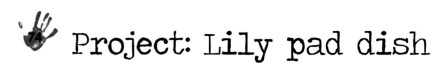

Project: Lily pad dish

This project echoes Palissy's watery theme by using a lily pad as the base for the dish design, but you can adapt any leaf shape that you want and decorate it in any pattern you like in any range of colors that you have at hand.

1 First make a template by drawing a lily pad on your cardboard and cut it out. Roll out your clay evenly to a size big enough for the leaf template to fit, and then cut around it with the plastic knife.

2 Press the real leaf onto your clay lily pad so that the veins make a pattern on the surface. Then shape the edges of the clay to form a dish. Place balls of newspaper under the sides to support the dish, and let it dry.

Piece of 8 ½ x 11-inch (Letter) cardboard

Pencil

Scissors

Board or old tray

Rolling pin

Plastic knife

Air-dry clay

Spray bottle filled with water

1 real leaf (any kind will do)

Newspaper

Acrylic or poster paints in dark green, blue, and white

1 medium and 1 fine paintbrush

3 Once dry, peel away the leaf and remove the newspaper supports. Paint the dish dark green and let it dry. Using your white paint and a fine paintbrush, draw in the vein patterning of the leaf and let dry.

4 Add a pattern of green, blue, and white (or any colors that you prefer) around the edges of the dish. Allow to dry. Your dish is now ready for the animal decorations that can be found in the next project.

Top tips

• Spray the clay with water to keep it moist.
• When rolling out the clay, lift it off the board once or twice to prevent sticking.
• You can speed up the drying process by using a hair dryer.

Project: Frog and shell decorations

This next project shows you how to make a frog and shells to go with your lily pad dish. Instead of a frog you could choose to make any of the other creatures on Palissy's dish (or something else that might sit on a lily pad, such as a dragonfly).

1 Start by making a sketch of the frog. Then make an oval shape for the body in clay. For the back legs, roll out a little clay, then fold and press the ends to make feet. Repeat this with shorter lengths for the arms.

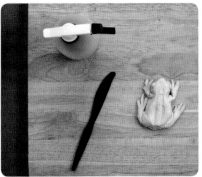

2 Attach the limbs to the body by smoothing over the clay to join it. Roll some balls of clay to make the bulging eyes and attach in the same way. Smooth over the frog with a wet finger to ensure that all parts are securely attached. Allow to dry.

3 Next, make a thin sausage shape about 4 inches (10 cm) long. Then roll the clay into a spiral to create the shell shape. Spray with water and press the joins lightly together without crushing the spiral pattern. Carve in extra pattern or detail with a tooth pick.

4 Paint your frog in your chosen color and allow to dry. Then add markings in yellow and white. Paint the shells white. Arrange your frog and shells on your dish and fix in place with glue. Finally cover the whole dish with a solution of glue and water.

Top tips

• As with the last project, you can keep the clay moist by spraying it with water.

• Take your time with the painting and build up the colors slowly and with care.

Woman with a Flowery Hat

Picasso created more than two thousand ceramic pieces. What was it about this media that so appealed to him?

Artist	Pablo Picasso
Nationality	Spanish
Made	1964

What's the story?

Picasso first met the potters Georges and Suzanne Ramié in 1946. For the next twenty years he spent his summers on the Côte d'Azur in France producing ceramics at their pottery studio. He found working with clay less stressful than creating paintings. He liked the malleable nature of the clay, the different textural effects that could be produced, and experimenting with glazes. He started with simple items, such as plates and dishes, and later moved on to more complex pieces.

Woman with a Flowery Hat is from Picasso's late period when he was inspired by Greek mythology, and his bold use of black against the red clay makes references to early Greek pottery. The woman in the hat is thought to be Jacqueline Roque, who was to become Picasso's second wife. She looks directly out at us, but her nose is seen in profile, which is a key characteristic of Picasso's Cubist style. The artist added patterned surface textures that help to create a sense of depth and makes shadows.

Another reason that perhaps Picasso enjoyed working with clay was because it matched his own sensual earthy character. Here his unglazed surface gives the work a sense of raw and unrefined energy; and Jacqueline, although she was a modern woman, is portrayed as an ancient goddess.

Think about ...

What is "slip"?
Slip is a mixture of clay and water that can be used to join clay pieces together or to decorate them. Colored slip is made by adding pigment and is applied to a piece before the clay has dried.

Why use a colored slip rather than a glaze?
The raw energy and drama of this piece is partly achieved by the use of a matte black slip against the bright red of the terra-cotta. Ceramics are often glazed, which is a special type of finish created by coating the clay in a kind of mineral paint, and then baking or "firing" it in a kiln to so that it becomes hard and shiny. Glazes come in many colors and can be bright as jewels. However if this piece were glazed, it would have lost the sense of simplicity and contrast that Picasso was trying to evoke.

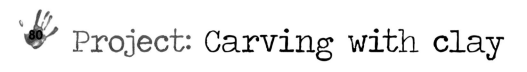

Project: Carving with clay

When Picasso made *Woman with a Flowery Hat* he worked on the clay when it was wet. Here we will see how a similar effect can be achieved by letting the clay dry a little and then carving into it with a variety of simple tools that you can find around the house.

1 Roll out the clay to a rectangle about 8 x 7 inches (20 x 18 cm). Cut away any excess pieces and set aside. Allow the clay to partially dry out (this might take a whole day, but you can speed the process with a hair dryer).

2 While the rectangle is drying use the pieces of excess clay to experiment with your tools and see the different effects you can produce. You can also practice sketching a face on the paper—think about what sort of hair, eyes, or hat your face will have.

3 When the clay rectangle is partially dry, you can begin to carve the shape of the face into the clay. Press lightly to start with and then, when you are happy with the effect, go a little deeper. Don't forget to make a background pattern.

4 Next, test your ink on a spare piece of clay to see how dark the color is, then paint in the face with the ink and paintbrush. Let dry, and then add a second coat of ink to any areas you want to stand out more.

Top tips

• Dry clay is fragile, so don't press too hard or it might break.

• If you don't have red clay you can paint the rectangle orange and let it dry before adding the black ink.

• Different widths and depths of line create a more dynamic look.

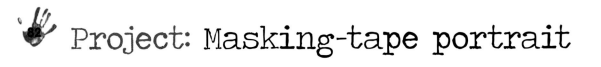

Project: Masking-tape portrait

The last project showed how carving into clay can create a sense of depth. Here you can try out a raised effect, by molding masking tape into a portrait. Using an everyday material such as tape also evokes the same simplicity as Picasso's portrait.

Sheet of 8 ½ x 14-inch (Legal) cardboard

Brown wrapping paper

Scissors

Pencil

Masking tape

Glue

Black pastel or crayon

Black felt-tip pens in different widths

1 Start by centering your cardboard in the middle of the brown paper. Make diagonal cuts in each corner of the paper. Fold over the edges and tape down with masking tape. Sketch a face like Picasso's lady on the brown paper.

2 Cut a length of masking tape about 8 inches (20 cm) long. Twist the tape and then stick it down onto the line of the face. Continue adding twists of tape around the lines of the face. Then move on to the hair and fill it in the same way.

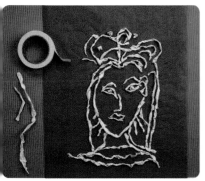

Top tip

Varying the height and thickness of your masking-tape twists will give more depth and dimension to your work.

3 Then move on to the features of the face. For the eyes you will need to make small balls of tape. Finally move on to the hat, keeping the shapes simple. If the masking tape starts to lift, stick it down with some glue and allow to dry.

4 Use pastel or crayon to color over the tape. Then fill in the finer details using your pens. You can add extra details, such as a frame, to complete your picture.

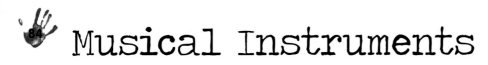

Musical Instruments

Musical themes were a popular subject for artists of the early part of the 20th century, and the Italian sculptor Leoncillo Leonardi (known just as "Leoncillo") was no exception.

Artist	Leoncillo
Nationality	Italian
Made	1948

What's the story?

Leoncillo's grandfather was a cabinetmaker, and this influenced young Leoncillo in his love of the applied arts. The early 20th century was a very turbulent time, with two World Wars, and the explosion of artistic movements during this period are a reflection of how people tried to cope with the turmoil.

Leoncillo, along with many artists of this period, explored many different styles and media. Yet, although the style of his works may be different, they all seem to be linked by a sense of restless energy—like a never-ending piece of music.

In the 1930s Leoncillo started experimenting with clay and toward the end of the decade he began to produce large-scale ceramic pieces in earnest, working with a variety of shapes, sizes, and colored glazes. He made this piece, *Musical Instruments*, in 1948. Try to imagine how this work would look in just one color; the effect would be of a purely abstract pattern. It is only the colors that define the instruments. However the use of clay and pastel glazes softens the colors and the lines, so that the instruments seem to blend and create a harmonious whole. Leoncillo was not interested in creating a realistic or refined image of some instruments. For him it is all about capturing the sounds and the emotions raised by the music itself.

Think about . . .

How do music and art go together?
A piece of music is composed of an arrangement of notes, and we also speak of the "composition" of a painting. Since the Renaissance, musicians and music-making have been popular subjects for artists. In the early 20th century artists such as Wassily Kandinsky and Piet Mondrian took this one step further and explored how the aural experience of hearing music could be expressed in visual terms.

What do you imagine when you look at *Musical Instruments*?
What kind of music do you think the instruments would play? Does it sound fast and happy? Or slow and somber? Does it make you want to dance? This is something to consider when choosing the instruments for your projects.

"I think these instruments would sound loud and fast."

Josie, age 7

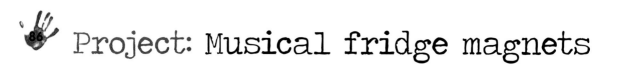

Project: Musical fridge magnets

For this project we are going to create fridge magnets with a musical theme. Instead of clay we will use salt dough, which is simple to make and easy to shape. You could copy Leoncillo's design or use the shapes of some your own favorite instruments.

1 Start by making your salt dough. Add the salt to the flour and slowly add the water, mixing with a wooden spoon. You need a firm dough that isn't sticky (so you may not need to add all the water). Cover and set aside in the fridge for a few hours.

2 Draw your chosen instruments on the cardboard. Cut them out and set aside. Roll out the dough, place your templates on it, and cut around them with the plastic knife. Place the dough instruments onto a baking tray lined with baking paper.

3 To make the music staff, roll out five pieces of dough to about 8 inches (20 cm). Place on the tray and trim the ends with a knife. Mold the staff so that it has a slight wave shape. Add a length of dough in the form of a treble clef. See Top Tips for baking instructions and ask an adult to help.

4 Paint your staff white and allow to dry. Paint your treble clef black. Paint your instruments in bright colors and allow to dry. Stick the clef onto the staff. Make a solution of glue and water and apply all over. When dry fix your magnets to the back.

You will need

2 cups of flour
1 cup of salt
¾ cup of water
2 tablespoons of vegetable oil
Bowl and wooden spoon
Thin cardboard
Pencil
Scissors
Rolling pin
Plastic knife
Baking tray/baking paper
Assortment of acrylic paints including black and white
2 fine paintbrushes
Glue
Stick-on magnets

Top tips

• If the dough is too sticky add more flour.
• Bake in the oven at 180° F for 10 minutes, remove, and let cool entirely.

Project: Harmony in blue

This next project takes its inspiration from the Cubist movement that heavily influenced Leoncillo. To help unify the image the background wash and papers are all in shades of blue. You can choose any color but remember to change the color of the background wash to match.

1 Draw an oval that fills your legal-size thick paper. Then apply a light blue wash around the outside of the oval. Cut up your sheet music into strips and paste into the oval leaving empty squares around the edges. Then color in the squares.

2 Next make a simple line drawing of an instrument on a piece of letter-size paper. Repeat this step for two other instruments and cut out so you are left with three templates.

Sheet of 8 ½ x 14-inch (Legal) thick paper

Pencil

Blue watercolor paint

Sponge or large paintbrush

3 pieces of sheet music

Scissors

Glue stick or glue

Oil pastel or crayons in blue, black, and white

3 pieces 8 ½ x 11-inch (Letter) paper

Blue-colored magazine pages, candy wrappers, wrapping paper, or wallpaper

3 Select a variety of blue papers, cut into small pieces, and glue them onto your instrument templates. Allow the glue to dry and trim the edges where needed.

4 Cut the instruments into pieces and stick them at random in the oval. Don't worry if the pieces don't fit perfectly. Finally highlight certain details, such as the guitar strings, in black or white crayon or pastel.

Top tips

• You can photocopy one sheet of music as many times as you need or print out sheet music from the internet.

• A print roller or rolling pin will help flatten and fix your work to the card.

llen Angele
Schlafwagen
Flugscheine
Platzkarten
en Kreditbriefe; reservieren
Gesellschafts-Reisen
Deutschlands und im A

5 Collage

The word *collage* comes from the French *coller*, which means "to glue." Any artwork that has items glued to it is a collage. People have used collage for hundreds of years to decorate walls, objects, pictures, photograph albums, boxes, and books. In the early 20th century, collage was used by modern artists as part of oil paintings, and then in pictures made completely out of pasted items, to create a new form of art. This type of collage, like Juan Gris's *The Bottle of Banyuls* and Kurt Schwitters's *Opened by Customs* was part picture, part sculpture, and completely new. Joseph Cornell explores another form of collage by collecting found objects in his *Untitled (Soap Bubble Set)*.

The Bottle of Banyuls

Juan Gris's collage of a bottle of wine sitting on a woven tabletop or tray was made with lots of different types of materials. Paper has been pasted on, oil and gouache paints have been used, and charcoal and pencil can be seen too.

Artist	Juan Gris
Nationality	Spanish
Made	1914

What's the story?

Gris was a Spanish artist who went to live in Paris when he was nineteen and stayed there for the rest of his life. Gris was friends with Pablo Picasso (they lived in the same building) and Georges Braque, two artists responsible for an art movement called Cubism. Juan Gris admired Picasso's and Braque's work and started painting in a Cubist style.

In Cubist paintings, people, landscapes, and objects look all broken up, as if they have been painted on a piece of glass that has shattered. This kind of Cubism was called Analytical Cubism—it took things apart and put them back together again so that you could see things from lots of different angles all at the same time. The objects in Gris's picture seem to lie down awkwardly when they should really be standing up.

Collage was an important part of Cubist art. Cubist artists experimented with sticking everyday items, such as wallpaper and oilcloth, onto canvas to make pictures that jutted out and became three-dimensional. It was as if the canvas was a tray and the Cubists were serving up real objects for you to look at. This kind of Cubism was called Synthetic Cubism—it stuck things together rather than took them apart. You can see Synthetic Cubism in Gris's picture as well.

Think about . . .

What is Banyuls?
Banyuls is a French sweet wine, drunk with dessert after a meal.

What is a "still life"?
The Bottle of Banyuls is a still life—a collection of objects chosen and arranged by the artist and then painted, drawn, or photographed.

Are the objects in the picture falling?
The glass in the picture sits solidly on the tabletop, but the bottle, newspaper, and pipe look as though they are falling off the edge of the surface of the picture. These objects have been given sharp angles that intersect with each other—this makes them look as if they are moving, even though this is a "still" life.

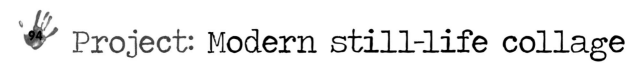

Project: Modern still-life collage

Create a still-life collage that uses modern materials to recreate *The Bottle of Banyuls* with a 21st-century look.

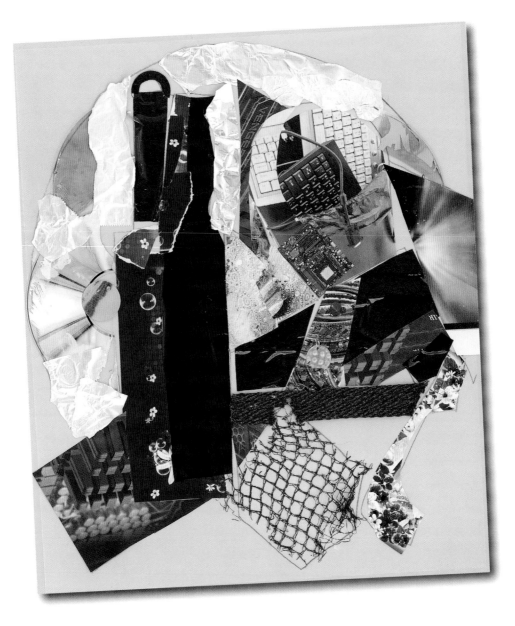

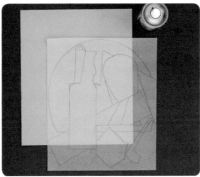

1 Ask an adult to photocopy and enlarge *The Bottle of Banyuls* (page 93). This photocopy will be your guide. Fix the tracing paper to the photocopy and draw the outlines of the objects in the picture.

2 Take your can of adhesive spray and spray lightly over the surface of the stiff cardboard, then carefully stick the tracing paper down on top.

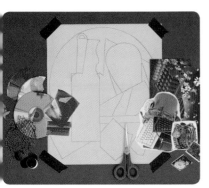

3 Use the masking tape to fix your cardboard-backed tracing paper to a table. Arrange and rearrange the things you have collected within the outlines of your drawing. Tear or cut the printouts to fit the outlines and background.

4 When you are happy with your composition, glue everything down. How different does your collage look from Gris's picture?

Top tip

Your collage doesn't have to be based on the painting. Sketch a simple outline of any object or scene you like and create a completely different still-life collage.

Project: Texture collage

Collages are not just about shapes—they are also about introducing different textures to pictures so that they become something you can feel as well as see.

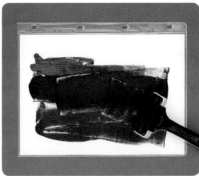

1 Cut a shape from baking paper for the middle of your picture. It can be anything you like—a heart, a question mark, a circle, a fish, or an arrow are some ideas.

2 Insert the piece of white paper into the plastic sleeve. Put three blobs of different-colored paint onto the plastic. Roll the paint out over the surface but not right up to the edges. Try to leave as much paint as possible on the sleeve.

You will need

Baking paper

Scissors

Piece of 8 ½ x 11-inch (Letter) white paper

Clear plastic sleeve

Acrylic paints

Small paint roller

Piece of bubble wrap

Net bag, the type used for packaging oranges or lemons

Paintbrush with a pointed end

Sheet of good-quality paper, smaller than the plastic sleeve

Felt-tip pens, chalks, or colored pencils

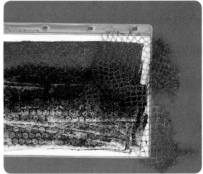

3 Place the bubble wrap somewhere on the paint. Press it down lightly and then lift it off again. You should be able to clearly see an imprint of the pattern.

4 Repeat step 3 using the net on a different section of the paint, to create another pattern.

5 While the paint is still wet, you can use the end of the paintbrush to draw in the paint, and add in any other details you like. Then place the parchment shape where you want it to be on the painted surface.

6 Lay your paper down on top of the sleeve. Rub the back to help transfer the paint. Lift off the paper. You should have a paint background with areas of texture and a clear shape left by the parchment. When the paint is dry, add any details you want with felt-tip pens, chalks, or colored pencils.

Top tips

Try making textures in paint with different objects. Here are some suggestions:
- corrugated cardboard
- old doilies
- bottle caps
- a comb
- balls of tin foil
- a ruler

Opened by Customs

This collage is about the size of a sheet of paper, but it manages to cram in German newspapers, Norwegian newspapers, a photograph, wrapping paper, customs labels, and a tissue-paper fruit wrapper. Schwitters also used oil paints, pencil, and crayons in the picture.

Artist	Kurt Schwitters
Nationality	German
Made	1937–38

What's the story?

Schwitters created his collage works using everyday objects such as train tickets, newspaper clippings, postage stamps, and discarded materials. He believed that anything could be considered art, and drew on the everyday objects for a constant source of inspiration.

This particular work was unnamed during Schwitters's lifetime, but his son Ernst later named it *Opened by Customs* because of the three German customs labels included at the top of the picture. They are stamped with the word "Hanover," the German city in which Schwitters was born, and the date, 3.8.37.

The collage is a snapshot of the artist's life in the few years before World War II began—it reflects the fact that he had to move from country to country to search for safety. The collage is full of words and items connected to travel and movement. In the left-hand corner you can see a Norwegian word that translates into English as "going." Brown paper, usually wrapped around packages before they're mailed, is stuck down in the middle of the picture. At the center, on white paper, is a list in German of words to do with travel —"baggage insurance," "sleeper car," "reservations," and "airline boarding pass."

Think about . . .

What other things did Schwitters use in his collages?
He used anything he could get to stick to a flat surface, such as bus passes, the soles of shoes, and pieces of floor coverings.

Who do you think the man in the photograph is?
Some people think that the photo of the man in a suit in the bottom-right corner represents Schwitters going off on his journeys.

Can you spot the fruit wrapper?
It is in the middle of the picture, slightly to the right. It is made of colorful tissue paper and would have been used to wrap fruit such as oranges. The writing on the wrapper tells us that it came from Spain.

Project: Themed collage

Making themed collages is a good way of focusing on a group of objects and papers to collect. You can also tell a story with a themed collage, just as Kurt Schwitters did with *Opened by Customs*. In this project, the subject is machines and technology to give a modern, futuristic feel to the collage.

1 Collect objects and images relating to your chosen subject —in this case, machines.

2 Find a piece of heavy cardboard to use as the base for your collage. It needs to be quite sturdy so that it can support the weight of the paper and objects you paste to it. Begin by placing all the biggest items you have collected onto the cardboard.

3 Once you are happy with the positions of the biggest objects, start to arrange the smaller pieces. You can link these items using themes, colors, or directions. Try different arrangements until you are happy with the way everything looks.

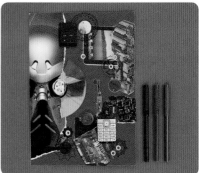

4 Now glue everything into position. Once all the objects are in position and the glue has dried, go over the spaces in between with paints, crayons, felt tips, or pencils.

Top tips

Here are some other suggestions for themed collages you can create:
- a day in my life
- my favorite season
- colors
- my best vacation
- castles
- music
- family
- my favorite city
- holidays
- hobbies

Project: Rolled-paper collage

Scrap paper taken from old magazines is an important ingredient of collage. This project shows you how to roll magazine paper into tubes that can be used to make pictures.

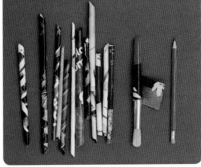

You will need

An old magazine

Ruler

Pencil

Scissors

Paintbrushes with different-sized handles, from thick to thin

Glue

Small paintbrush for use with the glue

Hand wipes

Scrap paper, the same size as the canvas

A mounted canvas, 8 ½ x 11-inch (Letter) or smaller

1 Using your pencil and ruler, draw squares and rectangles on the first page of the magazine. Holding four pages together, cut out the shapes to make multiple squares and rectangles. Repeat four or five times.

2 Wind a square or a rectangle tightly around the handle of a paintbrush. When you get to the end of the paper, with about ½ inch (1 cm) to go, dab some glue on and seal the roll.

3 Make lots and lots of rolls—this may give you sticky fingers, so keep using the hand wipes to keep your fingers free of glue. Using the scrap paper, arrange your tubes in patterns or make an actual picture —perhaps a landscape or a face, a heart or a skyscraper.

4 Trim the edges of the rolls to fill the spaces. Once you are happy with your arrangement, transfer the tubes to the canvas, sticking them down with glue.

Top tip

If you roll the paper around paintbrush handles of varying thicknesses, the tubes will be different widths, which will add extra levels to your picture.

Untitled (Soap Bubble Set)

Salvador Dalí described the art of Joseph Cornell as "the only truly surrealist work to be found in America." His innovative creations were hugely influential and inspired a generation of modern and contemporary artists.

Artist	Joseph Cornell
Nationality	American
Made	1949

What's the story?

Cornell (born in 1903) was famously reclusive and liked to stay out of the spotlight. He didn't talk much about his art and preferred to describe it as a kind of "white magic." He made a number of works like this one and called them "shadow boxes," which is a phrase used to describe the special cases used for displaying jewelry, coins, or other small objects. However in Cornell's hands the term seems infinitely more mysterious.

This work belongs to a series entitled *Soap Bubble Set*, and Cornell said all the boxes in this series were linked by themes of childhood and the universe (for instance the box's dark blue velvet lining is like the night sky and the white objects against it are like stars). A pipe, a ball, and cylindrical weights might look like random objects to us, but for Cornell there was a link. It has even been suggested that the pieces represent various members of his family. This unexpected grouping of objects gives the work a mysterious quality and leaves the viewer wondering what the links between them may be.

Cornell chose to use objects that other people had thrown away (he often found them while walking on the beach), which he then carefully painted and artfully arranged as if they were very precious and he was putting them on display in a museum.

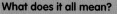 Think about

What does it all mean?
The reasons for selecting these particular objects are very personal to Cornell and only he knew exactly why he chose them, but he explained that some of the items reminded him of his childhood. The glass and ball suggest a cup-and-ball game, and the little clay pipe made Cornell think of blowing bubbles.

How would you describe it?
Cornell's work has been described as romantic, poetic, lyrical, and surrealist; what words would you use to describe his work?

What objects would you put into a special box?
What objects could represent your life or your feelings?

"I would put a picture of my dog in my box."
Oliver, age 7

Project: Magical boxes

In this project you can create "magic" like Cornell did, by shining a flashlight through colored cellophane to reveal some hidden cutout shapes. Our shapes are dragonflies and butterflies, but you can choose any theme you like.

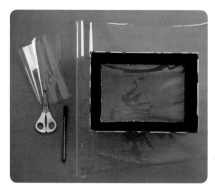

1 Cut away the base of the box leaving a 1 inch (2 cm) border, and paint the inside with black paint. When dry, lay the clear cellophane on your work surface and place your box squarely on top. Draw around the box and cut out the cellophane rectangle.

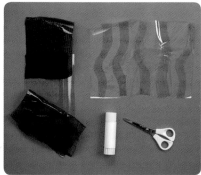

2 Cut your colored cellophane into shapes and stick onto the rectangle of clear cellophane, It doesn't matter if the pieces overlap. Continue until the rectangle is filled with colored cellophane.

3 Put glue around the border at the back of the box and stick down the rectangle to create a colored window effect.

4 Draw your chosen shapes onto the cardboard and cut them out. Apply small pieces of adhesive putty to your cutouts and gently press them onto the cellophane. Finally, shine a flashlight through the box to reveal your scene.

Top tips

• Candy often come wrapped in colored cellophane, so save up the wrappers!

• Try to match your cellophane colors to your chosen theme.

• If you don't have a colored box, you can cover the outside with wrapping paper or paint.

Project: Shadow box

Use a cereal box to create a frame for your "shadow box" and
decorate it in various ways. Before you start this project choose
a theme for the box and then find objects to hang and display
within it. Remember to choose objects that don't have an obvious
link, but have special a connection that will make sense to you.

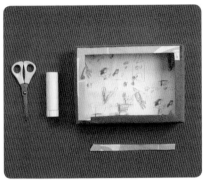

1 Measure a rectangle on one side of your cereal box leaving a 2 inch (4 cm) frame. Cut out the rectangle with scissors. Line the back of the box with pictures and glue into place. When complete apply a thin layer of glue all over and allow to dry.

2 Tape up the end of the box. Paint the box all over in your chosen colour and allow to dry, or cover it in wrapping paper. When dry, paint on a decorative frame or make one by adding strips of wallpaper or buttons. Allow to dry.

Ruler

Pencil

Empty cereal box

Scissors

Magazine pages or pictures to line the inside of the box

Glue

Masking tape

Medium paintbrush

Poster or acrylic paints

Wrapping paper (optional)

Needle

Thin metal wire

Newspaper

Medium thickness cardboard

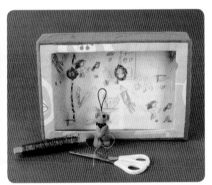

3 Make small holes at the top of the box with a needle. Cut lengths of wire according to how low you wish your objects to hang and wrap it around them. Pass the wire through the holes at the top and bend to secure.

4 Stuff newspaper inside the bottom of the box so that it reaches the bottom of the frame. Measure a length of cardboard and slip inside to form a shelf on top of the newspaper. Place your chosen objects on the shelf.

Top tips

• Try making your shelf slightly wider than the box so that it juts out.
• If you don't have any acrylic paint try adding glue to poster paint.

6 Textiles

In our daily lives we are surrounded by all forms of
textiles and textures—sofas, carpets, curtains, and,
of course, clothing. But it has only been in the 20th
century that textiles have been seen as an art form.
The pieces featured in this chapter show the wonderful
diversity and creativity that can be created with textiles,
from Alphonse Mucha's rich decorative lithograph
Young Girl with Flowers to Gunta Stölzl's experimental
Design for a Wall Hanging, and the bright and energetic
effects of Nina Shirokova's colorful paisley textile.

Young Girl with Flowers

These days we might see Alphonse Mucha's lovely lithograph as charming and beautiful rather than modern or groundbreaking. But when Mucha's work first appeared on the Paris art scene in 1895 it was seen as completely different to the art that had gone before.

Artist	Alphonse Mucha
Nationality	Czech
Made	1900

What's the story?

In Mucha's lithograph *Young Girl with Flowers* the figure is portrayed as being as natural as her floral surroundings. Like the exotic lilies that form a canopy around her, she too is lush and sensuous, an effect that is heightened by her loose clothes and free-flowing hair, something that would have been seen as very shocking to the previous generation of corseted Victorian women. Her bejeweled hair and exotic flowers put us in mind of faraway places and add an air of mystery. The image is produced on a silklike fabric, which adds to the richness and tactile nature. There is not one straight line in the image; it is made up of continuous, wavy lines, which give off a restless energy in contrast to the languid pose.

In real life the "Mucha" woman was best typified by the world-famous French actress Sarah Bernhardt, and fittingly it was she who gave Mucha a commission that made him a household name, to design a poster for her latest show. With "Gismonda" he succeeded in creating a poster that was completely different from others on the billboards. From the success of "Gismonda" he went on to receive many other commissions, including illustrated books, furniture, wallpaper, carpets, jewelery design, and calendars. His work was seen as capturing the mood of the moment, a spirit of reform and rebellion. It was given the name Art Nouveau, which in French means "new art."

Think about . . .

What marked out Art Nouveau as different to previous movements? Previous art movements focused on painting or architecture, but Art Nouveau embraced all the arts, including interior design, the decorative arts, fashion, and jewelry. This is demonstrated in the Mucha work by the fact that he uses different media.

What makes this work typical of the Art Nouveau style? If we examine Mucha's earlier work, we discover that we see the same type of woman portrayed with the same bejeweled hair and loose clothes, set against a backdrop of wild, exotic flowers. The way the woman is depicted in a very relaxed and languorous pose immediately tells us that it is a Mucha work. Compare this work with others of his of the same period and you will see how his figures are of a type.

"I like all the flowers around the lady.
She looks a lot like them."

Alice, age 11

Project: Lilies in a vase

For this next project we are going to create a vase of lilies using a variety of mixed media, including assorted fabrics and wallpaper. The colors and fabrics in this project have been chosen to reproduce the rich lushness of the original Mucha lithograph, and the patterns match the sinuous shapes typical of the Art Nouveau period.

1 Place your cardboard onto the center of the reverse side of the wallpaper, allowing a 1 inch (2 cm) border. Mark out each corner with a pencil. Make diagonal cuts at each corner of the wallpaper, fold back the excess paper, trimming if needed, and glue these down onto the cardboard.

4 With a pen or pencil sketch out a vase around the stems. This will act as your guide when you are sticking down your fabric strips.

2 Draw a lily flower template onto the paper and cut it out. Place it on one of the white felt squares. Draw around it with your felt tip, remove the template, and cut out. Repeat this step until you have enough lilies to fill two-thirds of your cardboard.

3 Cut some thin lengths of green felt for the stems. Use the remainder of the felt to draw and cut out some leaves. Arrange the stems and leaves on the wallpaper card and then stick them down. Now arrange your flower heads at the top of the stems and stick them down. Allow to dry.

5 Starting from the bottom of the vase, fill it in with your fabric strips, trimming where necessary, until the vase is complete. When you are happy with your arrangement of fabric, stick it down. Allow it to dry.

6 Cut off small pieces of pipe cleaner about 1 inch (2 cm) long, about three per flower, and curl them up slightly at one end. These will be the flower stamens. Stick the stamens onto each lily and allow to dry.

Top tip

The number of lilies you will need will vary according to the size of your cardboard, and you can cut longer pipe cleaner and fabric strip lengths to match a larger scale.

Project: Peacock pot

Of all the symbols most closely linked with the Art Nouveau movement, it was the peacock, with its exotic plumage and rich colors, that came to represent the style. For this project we are going to make a handy pencil-and-pen pot decorated in felt with a peacock motif.

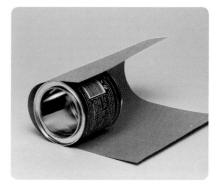

1 Place your can lengthwise at one end of your piece of paper and, holding the end, roll the can so that the paper wraps around it. Mark off the top and bottom of the tin where the two ends meet.

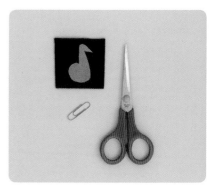

4 Draw your own design of a peacock body onto paper. Cut it out and attach it to a scrap of felt with a paper clip. Cut the body out of the felt, then stick the felt body onto the can, allowing enough space for the peacock's head plumes and legs. Press it down and allow it to dry.

You will need

Piece of 8 ½ x 11-inch (Letter) paper

A cleaned, empty can— the type with a lid used for storing hot chocolate; or a large yogurt tub

Pencil

Ruler

Scissors

Piece of felt, big enough to cover the can

Paper clips

Felt-tip pen

Glue

Length of braid or ribbon, ½ inch (1 cm) wide and long enough to go around the can twice

A small sheet of paper

Scraps of felt in a variety of colors

Sequins, any color

2 Using your ruler, join up your pencil marks to form a rectangle. Cut this out and attach it to your piece of felt with a paper clip. With your felt tip, carefully draw around the paper. Remove the paper and cut out the felt rectangle, discarding the rest.

3 Stick the felt to the can, using the glue, pressing down firmly. Measure out two lengths of braid by wrapping it around the can and cutting it to size. Using the glue, stick one piece around the top of the can and the other around the bottom. Allow it to dry.

5 To make the feathers, using your felt tip draw teardrop shapes of different sizes on different-colored scraps of felt or fabric and cut them out. Stick these all around the body of the peacock, the larger pieces first, then fit the smaller ones around them. Press them down and allow them to dry.

6 Glue the sequins onto the ends of the feathers, pressing them down, and allow them to dry. Add a smaller sequin to the peacock head for the eye. Using your felt-tip pen, draw on some legs and three head plumes.

Top tips

- For your background felt, choose a color that contrasts with your peacock colors.
- Don't use a can that has a ring-pull lid, as it can have sharp edges.

Design for a Wall Hanging

The design for this beautiful wall hanging was created in 1927 or 1928, and it marked a very key period for Gunta Stölzl. She went from being a junior master to a full master of weaving, the only woman at the Bauhaus (a German school of architecture and applied arts) to gain such status. Under her direction, the department became the most successful at the Bauhaus; she applied the new ideas of modern art—for example, abstraction and Cubism—to weaving, including experimenting with man-made fabrics.

Artist	Gunta Stölzl
Nationality	German
Painted	1927–8

What's the story?

Gunta Stölzl was studying at the Bauhaus in 1920. Her creativity, talent, and understanding of the technical side of weaving were soon realized. Before her appointment as director of weaving in 1927 the textile department at the Bauhaus was much neglected because it was seen as "woman's work."

She realized the importance of developing technical skills and insisted that her students had lessons in weaving techniques, dyeing, math, and geometry, combining a teaching and production workshop. We see these ideas being applied in the design for a wall hanging. The design itself is a bold composition of contrasting geometric shapes reflecting the work of the Cubists and the Art Deco movement. The bold shapes are equally offset by strong, contrasting colors so that, combined, there is an overall sense of dynamic movement and harmonious color.

This was most likely a design for a 1927/28 wall hanging, *Slit Tapestry Red/Green,* made using the Gobelin technique (see "Think about" box opposite) from a mixture of cotton, silk, and linen. Her contribution to modern art was that she revived and reestablished tapestries and weaving, demonstrating that it could be an art form.

Think about . . .

Just what makes Gunta Stölzl's wall hanging design so revolutionary and modern? Before the 1920s, textiles and embroidery were considered very much "women's work," but Stölzl demonstrates how these media can be considered an art form. She does this with her radical method of production (the Gobelin technique, see page 138) and by exploring "new textiles," and also in the reflection of the new art movements of Art Deco and Cubism.

Project: Cubist-inspired tapestry

Gunta Stölzl used the ideas of modern art in her work and experimented using new textiles. This art project reflects the work of the Cubists in the use of geometric shapes and of different types of textile. We'll use a weaving technique in which warp and weft threads are woven on a loom. The warps are the vertical strings through which the horizontal wefts will be woven.

1 Cut into the box lid at both ends, at ½ inch (1 cm) intervals, ½ inch (1 cm) deep. Tape the end of the string to the lid top, run it over through the first end cuts, then vertically across the underside of the lid, to the cut at the other end. Loop it through the next cut, then back down to the other end. Continue to the last cut, then cut the string and tape the end to the lid top again.

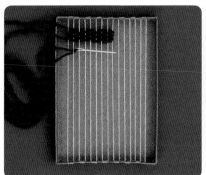

2 Mark out a design to follow on a piece of paper, indicating sections to fill with the different yarns and materials. Choose your first piece and tie the end to the first warp string. Thread the other end onto a needle and weave it horizontally over and under each warp. When you reach the last warp for that section, return back with the same weaving action.

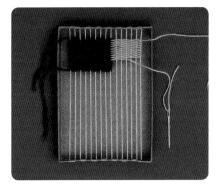

3 Once the shape for that section is complete, tie the end off on the last warp string. Select your next piece of string or other material and repeat the action.

4 When you have completed the tapestry, cut away the warp strings at the back of the lid, trim each string to make a fringe and knot each end to secure your weaving.

You will need

Shoebox lid, any size

Scissors

Masking tape or clear tape

Ball of string

A selection of yarns, ribbons, or strips of cellophane, colored plastic, or fabrics

Paper

Pencil

Top tips

- Make sure that the vertical strands of string are tight; otherwise the horizontal strands of yarn will not hold.
- After you complete each section, gently push up the weft threads so that the weave is tight.

Project: Patchwork collage

Gunta Stölzl's design has a patchwork quality about it. Patchwork is an ancient form of needlework that involves sewing together small pieces of cloth (in different colors, designs, or textures) into a larger design. In the past, patchwork was used as a way of using up leftover pieces of fabric, which traditionally would be made into quilts. In this project we are going to use textile scraps to create a patchwork collage.

You will need

Shoebox lid, or a piece of strong cardboard

An assortment of fabric scraps, buttons, wool, ribbons, wallpaper, candy wrappers

Scissors

Glue

Pencil and paper to draw a motif (optional)

1 Turn your box lid top-side down. Now take your selection of fabrics and try arranging them. You may need to trim the fabric scraps so that they interlock more easily. The idea is that they should fit together like pieces of a giant jigsaw.

2 When you are happy with your arrangement, glue all of the pieces down.

3 If you are using buttons or ribbons, it's best to lay these on top of the fabric scraps so that they stand out more and give greater depth to your collage.

4 We have added a dog shape to the collage, created by drawing a design on paper, then cutting it out and using it as a template. Cut the motif out of fabric and stick it on top of the base materials.

Top tips

- Use as many varieties of fabrics and textures as possible. This will make your collage more dynamic.
- Other ideas for motifs are hearts, flowers, birds, and so on.

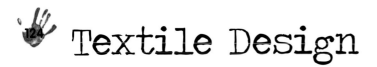

Textile Design

The vibrant colors and swirling abstract patterns of this textile design are best described as psychedelic—a word that was coined in the 1960s and refers to an altered state of mind, often involving drug use and hallucinations.

Artist	Nina Shirokova
Nationality	Russian
Painted	c.1960

What's the story?

Nina Shirokova, a Russian-born artist, studied art and textile design at the Moscow Textile Institute between 1956 and 1962. In the Soviet Union at the time art was expected to further socialist ideology. However, under the tutelage of her nonconformist instructor Eliy Bulyutin, Shirokova was able to flourish artistically—free to draw and paint beyond the restrictions of Soviet art. This textile design, which she created in 1960, reflects that freedom: bright reds, pinks, greens, and blues jostle and overlap each other in a chaotic pattern. The textile is also reminiscent of tie-dye, a method and style of fabric dyeing that became popularized in the 1960s hippie movement but that dates as far back as the 6th century CE.

Despite the apparent randomness of the pattern, if you look carefully you will notice that one shape occurs repeatedly: the enlarged teardrop, which went on to become known as the paisley pattern. This shape is originally Persian, dating back to the year 224 CE. In the West this design became known in the 18th century, when British sailors from the East India Company began bringing back cashmere shawls featuring the paisley motif. They became so popular that the Scottish town of Paisley started producing their own versions.

During the 1960s the design became associated with the psychedelic style. Fender Guitars even produced a pink paisley version of their Telecaster guitar. This textile demonstrates that while art and design can appear strikingly modern, it may well be based on a reinvention of an ancient method or theme.

Think about . . .

How has this textile reinvented ancient ideas to create something new and modern?
The teardrop design can be found in ancient Persian textile designs, an abstract combination of flora and fauna that represented life and eternity. This textile has taken that theme but transformed the idea with bright, fluorescent colors that can be associated with the psychedelic movement of the 1960s.

How would you create a design with ancient and modern themes?
Pick a favorite period from history. For example, you might choose the Celtic or Aztec era. Look at some of the objects from that period, such as jewelery or pottery, and look at the recurring themes and patterns. Then consider how you might reuse these designs with a modern twist: perhaps using completely different colors or modern materials.

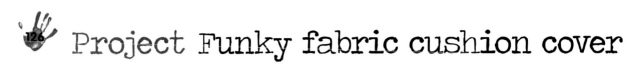
Project Funky fabric cushion cover

Taking the classic teardrop paisley shape as its starting point, this fabric-painting project offers endless variations using different techniques, paints, and tools. A plain cushion cover is used here, but if you don't have one, an old pillowcase will work just as well.

1 Draw several paisley teardrop shapes on your piece of cardboard and then cut them out.

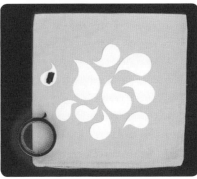

2 Arrange the pieces of cardboard on the cushion cover. These can be in a pattern or in a random layout. When you are happy with the arrangement, stick the pieces down with tack or tape.

3 Wet the toothbrush, load it up with paint, and hold it over the practice piece of paper. Pull your finger toward you, across the bristles—this will make the paint spray away from you. Repeat this step over the cushion cover.

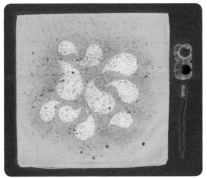

4 Clean your brush and repeat step 3 with another color. Continue until you have used as many colors as you like. When the paint is dry, remove the cardboard stencils and stuff the cover with a cushion insert.

You will need

Large piece of thin cardboard

Pencil

Scissors

Plain light-colored fabric cushion cover, any size

Poster tack or double-sided tape

Toothbrush

Cup of water

Selection of fabric paints in bright colors

Containers for paint

Piece of paper for practice

Cushion insert, the right size for the cover

Top tips

• You could also use water-based paints, but remember that they are not permanent and may stain other fabrics.

• You could cut out man-made sponges into teardrop shapes and use them as stampers.

Project: Tie-dyed T-shirt

This tie-dye project seems like a natural partner to the psychedelic paisley textile. The method used here involves wetting the fabric and scrunching it up before applying the dye. This will give a greater variation in shades and color tones.

1 Wearing gloves and an apron, wet your T-shirt in the bucket of water and wring it out so that it is damp. Place it on a flat surface protected by an old towel.

4 Add the salt to the water in the bucket and soak the T-shirt in it for 30 minutes. Remove from the water and squeeze out the excess.

2 Place two fingers in the center of the T-shirt and wrap the T-shirt around your fingers in a circular motion. Keep repeating this action until all the material is gathered in, resembling a large bun.

3 Remove your fingers from the center and crisscross the rubber bands across the T-shirt. The effect should look like slices of cake.

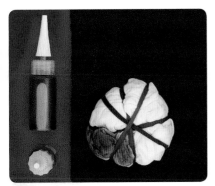

5 Apply the dye colors to the "cake slices," alternating the colors and making sure there is no white left. When you have finished, place the T-shirt in a plastic bag and leave for 24 hours.

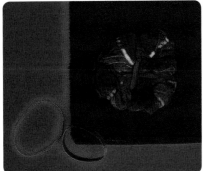

6 Remove the T-shirt from the bag and run it under the faucet, first warm then cold, until the water runs clear. Cut away the elastic bands then hand-wash and line-dry your T-shirt. It's now ready to wear.

Top tips

• Apply the dye slowly and don't oversaturate the fabric.
• You can use this tie-dye method to create other objects as well, such as scarves or linen napkins.

Artist biographies

Ai Weiwei

1957–

Chinese

Ai Weiwei is a Chinese artist who makes installations out of everyday objects such as bicycles, vases, wooden stools, or schoolbags. He likes to make works that surprise or amaze people, and in doing so encourages them to think about what his artworks might mean. For example, he once made an installation by filling the Turbine Hall in London's Tate Modern with millions of tiny sunflower seeds. And although each of the seeds looked real, they had in fact been specially made from porcelain. The artist wanted people who visited the gallery to think about the work that had gone into making such a huge installation, and to also think about how and where other everyday household objects are made or come from.

Ai Weiwei is also a photographer, performance artist, architect, filmmaker, and political activist. He once made an artwork in which he dropped a very valuable antique vase on purpose, to make people think about the value of art, authenticity, and China's cultural heritage.

Umberto Boccioni

1882–1916

Italian

Umberto Boccioni was a sculptor, painter, and writer at the heart of the Futurist movement. He is famous both for his colorful paintings and his sculptures.

The artist spent his childhood in Forlì, Genoa, and Padua, and later moved to Rome in 1899, where he became interested in painting. He made friends with the painter Gino Severini (1883 –1966), and together they visited the studio of an artist named Giacomo Balla

(1871–1958), who showed them his experiments in painting movement and encouraged them to try out his techniques. Balla also suggested looking at the new science of photography to better understand form and movement.

In 1909 or 1910 Boccioni met the writer Filippo Tommaso Marinetti (1876–1944), and together with their friends they formed a highly influential group called the Futurists. The group published a document explaining how they wanted to change the way art was made and understood. In particular they glorified modern technology and its speed, brute force, and energy. There is always a lot of movement in Futurist art.

In July 1915, Boccioni and many other Futurist artists went to fight in World War I, but only a year later he was killed in a cavalry training exercise.

Louise Bourgeois

1911–2010

French American

An artist and sculptor, Louise Bourgeois was born in Paris where her parents ran a studio that repaired antique tapestries. She started studying mathematics at the Sorbonne university in Paris, but swapped to study art instead.

A little later she married an American curator and art historian named Robert Goldwater and moved with him to New York in 1938. During World War II many people fled from Europe to the safety of the United States, and Bourgeois was able to work with and learn from great European artists such as Joan Miró (1893–1983) and André Masson (1896–1987) among others.

Bourgeois was interested in the work of contemporary abstract artists, but tended to avoid abstraction in her own work. Her pieces are often autobiographical and express themes of worry and loneliness that had been part of her childhood. This type of art is called confessional art.

She is famous for her abstract sculptures and installations, the most famous of which are her spider structures. The largest of the spiders is called *Maman*, (French for "Mommy"), which is over 30 feet (9 meters) high and is displayed outside the Guggenheim Museum in Bilbao, Spain.

Alex Chinneck
1984–

British

Alex Chinneck is an artist who likes to work on a large scale, and his sculptures often feature buildings. He has said that he was inspired to work with architecture by Rachel Whiteread's *House* (1993, see page 135), an installation in which the artist created a concrete cast of a building.

Chinneck also likes to surprise people, and his works often incorporate mind-bending visual effects that appear to cheat the laws of gravity or fool the eye. In 2012 in a work called *Telling the Truth Through False Teeth* he cut out 1,248 pieces of glass to make 312 identical smashed windows. He then fitted these windows into the front of a derelict factory in London so it looked as if each window had been broken in exactly the same way. In 2013 he created an installation called *Under the Weather but Over the Moon*, which made a building look as though it had been turned upside down, complete with upside down doors and windows. In 2014 in London's Covent Garden, Chinneck made a work called *Take My Lightning but Don't Steal My Thunder* (2014), in which he made a building look like it was floating in midair.

Joseph Cornell
1903–1972

American

Joseph Cornell was a sculptor, filmmaker, and writer. He led a very reclusive life and chose not to speak much about his art; however he is now celebrated as America's finest Surrealist artist.

After leaving university in 1921, Cornell became a salesman for a textile company in New York, but he continued to take a great interest in art. He very much admired the French painter Odilon Redon (1840–1916), an artist who belonged to the Symbolist movement and included unusual or unexpected images in his paintings that were intended to symbolize his thoughts or feelings—an idea that very much influenced and inspired Cornell.

In 1931, Cornell lost his job at the textile company and decided to show some of his own artworks to a gallery in New York. Through the gallery owner, Julien Levy, Cornell was introduced to the great French Surrealist artist Marcel Duchamp (1887–1968) in 1934, whom he greatly admired.

For his first exhibition in 1932 Cornell developed his iconic "shadow boxes"—small glass-fronted cases that he filled with unusual objects that he had found. Although the objects are seemingly unrelated there is often a poetic or symbolic relationship between them.

In the 1960s Cornell experienced intense grief at the deaths of his brother and mother. His own health declined, and he died in 1972, just a few days after his sixty-ninth birthday.

Donatello

*c.*1386–1466

Italian

Donatello was a sculptor from Florence, Italy, who lived during the early Italian Renaissance and is considered second only to Michelangelo in his skill and talent as a sculptor. As a boy Donatello started working as a goldsmith, which introduced him to handling and manipulating different kinds of metals. This experience would prove invaluable during his career as a sculptor. He trained under the artist Lorenzo Ghiberti (1378–1455), until he began receiving commissions of his own from wealthy patrons in Florence. His popularity continued throughout his life, during which time he created many sculptures. His best known works include a statue of a knight riding a horse, known as the *Gattamelata*, which can be seen in the Italian city of Padua, and also a remarkable statue of the boy David, a biblical hero who fought and killed the giant Goliath. The figure of David was very important to the people of Florence, who identified strongly with the young, underdog who stood up to a giant with courage, strength, and confidence.

Juan Gris

1887–1927

Spanish

Juan Gris was a painter and sculptor during the birth of Cubism. He was born in Spain, where he studied mechanical drawing, but he then moved to France, where he lived for most of his life. It was there that he painted a portrait of Picasso in the Cubist style in 1912. Gris painted with bright, harmonious colors and often used collage as his medium. He developed his style into synthetic Cubism—a style of Cubism which is more generalized, simplified, and flatter. In 1924, he designed ballet sets and costumes for Sergei Diaghilev (1872–1929) and the famous Ballets Russes. He also gave lectures on aesthetic theories. His preference for order influenced the style of the painter Amédée Ozenfant (1886–1966) and architect Le Corbusier (1887–1965), and made Gris an important exemplar of the postwar "return to order" movement.

Yayoi Kusama

1929–

Japanese

Yayoi Kusama is an avant-garde sculptor, painter, and novelist. She started to paint using polka dots and nets as motifs at around age ten, and created fantastic paintings in watercolors, pastels, and oils. Her trademark style includes psychedelic colors and patterns, especially polka dots. A precursor of the Pop Art, minimalist, and feminist art movements, Kusama influenced contemporaries such as Andy Warhol (1928–1987) and Claes Oldenburg (see below).

In the late 1950s she exhibited large paintings, soft sculptures, and environmental sculptures using mirrors and electric lights in the United States. In the late 1960s she staged many events such as body-painting festivals, fashion shows, and antiwar demonstrations. She also launched media-related activities such as film production and newspaper publication. More recently she began to create open-air sculptures and murals.

Her shows and exhibitions have taken place all over the world from the United States to France, Japan to Portugal. She has won several awards, such as the French Ordre des Arts et des Lettres (Officier), the Nagano Governor Prize (for her contribution in encouragement of art and culture) in 2003, the National Lifetime Achievement Award in 2006, and the Order of the Rising Sun, Gold Rays in 2006. In 2004, her solo exhibition *KUSAMATRIX* in Tokyo drew 520,000 visitors.

Leoncillo
1915–1968
Italian

Leoncillo Leonardi was born in Spoleto, Italy, in 1915. He was a shy child, and as a teenager he spent a lot of time alone carving and shaping clay blocks. He studied art in Perugia before moving on to the Academy of Fine Arts in Rome, but the artist would later explain that it was the years he spent as manager of a provincial pottery factory in an Umbrian village that were his real education in the art of ceramics. His work during this early period was influenced by Futurist artists, such as Umberto Boccioni (see page 130).

He went back to Rome in 1942 to teach ceramic art and was involved with the Resistance fighting against Benito Mussolini and the Italian Fascists during World War II. After the war in 1946 he joined the group Fronte Nuova delle Arti (the "New Art Front") who wanted to move Italian art away from the parameters and ideals created under the dictatorship of Mussolini.

Leoncillo (he chose to be called by his first name alone) had many solo and group exhibitions, and has an institute named after him in Italy.

Alphonse Mucha
1860–1939
Moravian (present-day Czech)

Alphonse Mucha shot to fame in Paris when he created "Gismonda," an advertising poster featuring Sarah Bernhardt, a famous actress of the time. The artist applied his style (using pastel colors, flowers, and often depicting beautiful women crowned with decorative halos) to paintings, posters, advertisements, book illustrations, jewelery, carpets, wallpapers, and much more. It soon became known as Art Nouveau, and was a radical change from much of the other art of the time.

Mucha always resented that he had become famous because of commercial art. He claimed that art should have a spiritual basis. He spent the last decades of his life working on the *Slav Epic*, a series of twenty paintings depicting the struggles and achievements of the Slav people.

Claes Oldenburg
1929–
Swedish American

Claes Oldenburg was born in Stockholm but has spent most of his life in the United States. He is a sculptor and likes to make art that does something different with ordinary objects. He has made figures, signs, and objects out of rough materials such as papier-mâché and sacking, and chooses to draw and construct everyday objects, such as light switches, lipsticks, typewriters, and binoculars.

In the 1960s he was associated with the Pop Art movement, a group of artists who found their inspiration in popular sources, such as advertising, packaging, or everyday items such as food and

newspapers. Oldenburg is well known for his "soft sculptures" in which he recreated commonplace items in soft, pliable materials at several times their normal size. In 1962 he made a giant hamburger, complete with bun and pickle, that is 6 feet (2 meters) wide.

Oldenburg is perhaps best known for his "large-scale projects," which are giant public art installations, often made in collaboration with his wife, Coosje van Bruggen (1942–2009).

Bernard Palissy

c.1510 – c.1590

French

Bernard Palissy, who was born and worked in France, had a diverse range of talents and interests despite never having any formal education. He is principally known for his work in the natural sciences and ceramics. As a Protestant, Palissy was outspoken about his religion and consequently ended up in prison, where he died after being condemned to death.

Palissy's first work was glass painting, but through his travels he discovered rustic-ware ceramics, and switched from glass painting to creating and designing ceramics. His style is identifiable by the plant, animal, and mythological designs he used to decorate ceramic plates and other dishes, as he did not sign his ceramics. Instead of a pottery wheel Palissy most likely used a mold to create his ceramics. His most famous commission was to create a ceramic grotto for the queen of France, Catherine de Médicis.

Pablo Picasso

1881–1973

Spanish

One of the most important and famous artists in history, and possibly the most important artist of the 20th century, the Spanish-born Pablo Picasso was a prolific artist who worked in painting, sculpting, print-making, and ceramics, as well as being a poet, stage designer, and playwright. Picasso trained at the Royal Academy of San Fernando as a teenager before moving to Paris, where he was key to the development of a new and innovative artistic style called Cubism, which was to transform modern art.

Picasso is also known as an early practitioner of "constructed sculpture" or "assemblage," a kind of three-dimensional collage in which an artist brings together a collection of objects. Picasso is more often thought of as a painter than a sculptor, but his innovation in both ceramics and sculpture was also highly influential. Picasso created an estimated 1,880 paintings and 1,220 sculptures during his life, and his best-known work is probably the giant canvas known as *Guernica* (Museo Reina Sofia, Madrid, Spain), which is over 25 feet (7 meters) long.

Kurt Schwitters

1887–1948

German

Kurt Schwitters was an artist, poet, and sculptor who created works in various media, including typography, graphic design, and collage. Schwitters took part in different 20th-century art movements, such as Constructivism and Surrealism, and was influenced by Cubism.

Kurt Schwitters lived and worked in Germany and was a part of the avant-garde art scene there. In 1918 he started making abstract collages, which he called "Merz"—he said that "Merz" meant "the art of everything." Schwitters's Merz collages are made of found objects—any objects he found lying around. He applied his Merz principles, using found objects and collage-like structures, to six rooms in his home in Hanover. He called these rooms the "Merzbau."

Schwitters fled Germany for Norway in 1937 to escape the Nazis. He escaped the German invasion of Norway by catching the last fishing boat to leave for Scotland. He died in England in 1948.

Nina Shirokova

1934–

Russian

Nina Ivanovna Shirokova was born in Tarusa, a city in western Russia. Shirokova loved to draw from an early age, and at twenty-two she studied at the Moscow Textile Institute (currently the Moscow State Textile University), specializing in textile design. Eliy Bulyutin, an instructor at the Textile Institute, greatly influenced Shirokova during her studies and for many years afterward. With his guidance, Shirokova was able to explore her craft and break away from the Social Realist tradition on which Soviet art was grounded.

In the 1960s, Shirokova worked in both industrial and interior design, drafting plans for one-room apartments and passenger airplane interiors. She also designed a series of scarves for a textile manufacturer. But beyond textile and architectural design, Shirokova is a skilled artist who uses vibrant colors and bold strokes to capture landscapes, still lifes, nudes, and portraits.

Gunta Stölzl

1897–1983

German

Gunta Stölzl was a German textile artist who was key in developing the weaving department of the Bauhaus school. Because of her work, she progressed to Bauhaus Master in 1927 but was dismissed for political reasons four years later. Stölzl applied modern art to textiles, experimented with new, more modern materials, and made sure her work was functional as well as visually pleasing. To do this, she applied technical sciences, such as mathematics, to her art, and encouraged all her students to do the same.

Rachel Whiteread

1963–

British

Rachel Whiteread makes sculptures and installations that often feature concrete casts of empty spaces, for example the spaces underneath chairs. In *House* (1993), Whiteread's most famous work, she poured concrete into a Victorian house that was going to be demolished and let it set hard. Then she chipped away the walls and roof of the house that surrounded the concrete so that only the concrete remained. The concrete preserved an impression of everything that had been left on the walls out the house, such as fireplaces and wallpaper.

Where to see the art in this book

Unknown, *Bronze Figure of a Running Girl*, British Museum, London, United Kingdom

Donatello, *Annunciation Tabernacle,* Church of Santa Croce, Florence, Italy

Louise Bourgeois, *Maman*, Guggenheim Museum, Bilbao, Spain

Claes Oldenburg, *Trowel*, Fundação de Serralves, Porto, Portugal

Umberto Boccioni, *Unique Forms of Continuity in Space*, Museo del Novecento, Milan, Italy (casts of this work are also on display at the Tate Modern, London, United Kingdom, and the Museum of Modern Art, New York, United States)

Yayoi Kusama, *The Tulips of Shangri-La*, Lille, France

Bernard Palissy, *Dish with a Snake*, Wallace Collection, London, United Kingdom

Pablo Picasso, *Woman with a Flowery Hat*, Metropolitan Museum of Art, New York, United States

Leoncillo, *Musical Instruments*, Galleria Arco Farnese, Rome, Italy

Kurt Schwitters, *Opened by Customs*, Tate Modern, London, United Kingdom

Alphonse Mucha, *Young Girl with Flowers*, Musée d'Orsay, Paris, France

Gunta Stölzl, *Design for a Wall Hanging*, Victoria & Albert Museum, London, United Kingdom

The works shown here by Ai Weiwei, Alex Chinneck, and Rachel Whiteread were created as temporary installations. These and other works by the artists, however, appear regularly in different exhibitions and displays. Visit the artists' own websites or those of their galleries to see where their works might be shown near you.

Glossary

A

Abstract art: Art that doesn't look like recognizable objects or people in the world, and instead uses shapes, colors, forms, or even marks and scratches to suggest an artist's ideas or feelings. Many art movements of the 20th century were abstract and a lot of today's art is abstract. (Art that is made to look like things, people, or places you *can* recognize is described as "realist;" see page 139.)

Art Deco: A style of interior decoration, design, jewelry, and architecture that was at its height in the 1930s and was usually characterized by geometrical shapes and stylized natural forms.

Art Nouveau: A style of art and architecture of the 1890s, characterized by swelling, sinuous outlines and stylized natural forms, such as flowers and leaves.

Annunciation: The announcement by the angel Gabriel to the Virgin Mary that she is pregnant with the Christ child as described in the Bible in *Luke (1:26–38)*. The Annunciation is a popular theme in Western art and was particularly favored during the Renaissance (see page 139), when it was depicted by Sandro Botticelli, Leonardo da Vinci, Raphael, and Donatello (see page 18), among many others.

assemblage: Art that is made by assembling a group of objects or materials. Sometimes the objects have a clear theme—as in the works of the artist Arman (1928–2005), who collected hundreds of cars, watches, or match boxes—and sometimes they have no obvious relationship at all.

avant-garde: A term often used to describe a group of artists, musicians, or writers working with new, experimental, or innovative ideas, techniques, and methods. It comes from the French word for "advance guard," literally meaning "those who go before."

B

bronze: A term that can refer to a yellowish-brown alloy (a mixture of the metals) made from copper and tin, or the sculptures or decorative pieces that are created from it. Bronze has been a favorite medium (see page 138) of sculptors since the ancient Greeks, and remains so to this day.

C

Classical: A word used to describe items or ideas relating to ancient Greece or Rome, or the literature, art, and culture of those eras. Artists of the Renaissance (see page 139) looked back to the Classical period as a golden age of art, and were highly influenced by the skills and techniques of the time.

collage: Stemming from the French term *coller* (meaning "to glue"), collage is a method of making art in which the piece is assembled using different materials, objects, and shapes. Collage can describe both the technique and the artwork that is created from it. Collage is often made by cutting up papers, photographs, or fabric and then sticking the pieces down onto a supporting surface, but the term can also be applied to collections of objects that are placed together, as in the works of Joseph Cornell (see page 104).

composition: The arrangement of the different elements in a picture such as the colors, perspective, objects, or people depicted.

constructed sculpture: See *assemblage*.

Cubism: A style of art that was developed by Pablo Picasso (see page 78) and Georges Braque (1882–1963) in the early 20th century. An art critic, Louis Vauxcelles, named the Cubist movement by noticing that their pictures were "full of little cubes." In its first phase, between 1908 and 1912, Cubism showed things from lots of different angles at the same time, which was called "Analytical Cubism." Everyday objects were broken down into basic shapes, taken apart, and put back together again in a disjointed way, to represent an object from lots of different angles at the same time. The second phase was called "Synthetic Cubism," active between 1912 and 1919, which used collage to depict objects and people, incorporating bits of newspaper, fabric, sheet music, magazines, and books. Synthetic Cubism stuck objects together, rather than pulled them apart. After 1916 Braque worked by himself to develop his art and Picasso moved on to drawing and painting in other ways.

Glossary

D

dynamic: Scientists refer to something that is constantly changing or moving as dynamic (which is why it is sometimes used to mean enthusiastic, energetic, or exciting). The term can also refer to a force that stimulates such a change or motion, so when someone talks about the dynamics of an artwork they are thinking about the different elements within the piece (the colors, textures, composition, etc.) and how they effect and energize each other.

Duchamp, Marcel: (1887–1968) French painter and sculptor whose work is associated with Cubism, conceptual art, Dada, and Surrealism. He was highly influential during his career and has continued to inspire generations of contemporary artists. In 1913 he created the first of his "readymades"—ordinary objects designated as works of art by the artist. His earliest readymades included a bicycle wheel mounted on a wooden stool and a snow shovel entitled *In Advance of the Broken Arm* (1915). Duchamp also used his readymades as symbols of his private thoughts and feelings.

F

fiberglass: A reinforced plastic material composed of glass fibers embedded in a resin matrix. Glass fibers had been made for a very long time, but they were brittle and hard to work with. It was only in the 1930s that the product known as fiberglass began to be mass produced, and its lightweight but strong form revolutionized the possibilities of sculpture.

fine art: Art that is created purely for aesthetic purposes, not for any practical use.

Futurism: An Italian art movement of the early 20th century that produced paintings, sculptures, textiles, ceramics, interior design, literature, architecture, music, and industrial design. The Futurists were led by Filippo Tommaso Marinetti (1876–1944), a writer who laid out the principles of the movement in the *Futurist Manifesto*, first published in 1909. The Futurists hated the art of the past and were interested in all of the wonders of the modern industrial age, such as speed, machines, airplanes, cars, and motorcycles. The Futurists believed that youth and violence should be praised above all the achievements of the past.

G

Gobelin technique: A complex weaving technique that differs from others in that the weft thread does not stretch across the full length of the piece; a different one is used for each section of the fabric.

I

installation: A three-dimensional art exhibit that is constructed within a gallery or space, and that alters the way that space is experienced.

L

lithograph: A form of print made from lithography; a method of printing from a metal or stone surface on which the printing areas are not raised but made ink receptive as opposed to repellent.

M

manifesto: The public declaration of a group's motives, policies, and aims. Manifestoes are usually political and are often published by political parties before an election so that voters might decide whether to vote for them. During the 20th century many artists adopted the technique as a way of declaring their presence and ideas; for example the Futurists first published their manifesto in 1909, and Albert Gleizes (1881–1953) and Jean Metzinger (1883–1956) captured the essence of Cubism in 1912.

medium: The material or form chosen by an artist in which to create their work. Watercolor, fiberglass, clay, or wool are all different kinds of medium. The plural of medium can be either "mediums" or "media," and when an artwork is created from different kinds of medium it is described as "mixed media."

Modern: The word *modern* is often used to describe any artwork, style, or movement that moves away from classical and traditional forms. When people say "modern art" or "modern architecture," they often simply mean things that were created in the 20th century or later. However, the terms "Modernist" or "Modernism" usually refer to a particular development in Western art and literature that began in the late 19th century and lasted until the 1950s and 60s. Modernists deliberately rejected the styles of the past and celebrated innovation and experimentation to better reflect the realities of their daily lives.

P

perspective: The skill of being able to draw or paint an object on a two-dimensional surface, such as a piece of paper, so that it looks three-dimensional. During the Renaissance, artists worked out mathematical formulas for perspective.

plinth: Usually a heavy base supporting a statue or vase, but a plinth can describe any surface or box on which a sculpture stands or is presented.

Pop Art: A mainly British and American art movement of the 1950s that used mass-produced popular images, such as those commonly found in advertising and commercial techniques to make high-brow art. Famous Pop Artists include Eduardo Paolozzi (1924–2005), Peter Blake (b.1932), Andy Warhol (1928–1987), Jasper Johns (b.1930), Robert Rauschenberg (1925–2008), and Roy Lichtenstein (1923–1997).

polyethylene: This is a plastic that is used in everyday objects such as plastic bags and bottles.

primary colors: The three basic colors, red, yellow, and blue, from which all other colors can be made, but which themselves cannot be made by mixing any other colors. The combination of any two primary colors is called a secondary color.

psychedelic: When referring to art and textiles, it means having intense, vivid colors or a swirling abstract pattern.

R

realism: Generally *realism* means art that is painted, drawn, or sculpted to look very like the object or person it is depicting. However it can also specifically refer to art from the 19th century in which artists chose their subjects from everyday life and depicted them in a very natural way (before this time people in art were often shown only on special occasions or when wearing their best clothes). Art that is intentionally made not to look like things, people, or places that you can recognize is described as abstract (see page 137).

relief: A method of carving, sculpting, or stamping in which the design stands out from the surface. When the design stands out a long way from the background it is called high relief, but when there is only a little difference between them it is called low relief.

Renaissance: Europe saw a remarkable flourishing in art, architecture, and literature between the 14th and the 16th centuries. Historians called it the Renaissance (from the French word meaning "rebirth") because artists of the period rediscovered a host of skills and techniques that had been lost following the decline of the ancient Greek and Roman civilizations. The stars of the early Renaissance were artists such as Donatello (see page 18) and Sandro Botticelli (1444/5–1510), who worked under the patronage of wealthy bankers in the city of Florence. The Renaissance reached its peak in a very short period that lasted from about 1500–1530, which is now known as the High Renaissance. These years saw the creation of some of the best-known artworks in all art history: the *Mona Lisa* by Leonardo da Vinci (1452–1519), the Sistine Chapel ceiling by Michelangelo (1475–1564), and the frescoes in Stanza della Segnatura in the Vatican by Raphael (1483–1520). Thereafter the Renaissance dissolved into myriad styles and schools, such as Mannerism, Baroque, Rococo, and neoclassicism.

S

sculpture: The art of making two- or three-dimensional realist or abstract forms, especially by carving stone or wood or by casting metal or plaster.

Sparta: A city in the southern Peloponnese in Greece. It was a powerful city-state in the 5th century BCE, defeating its rival Athens in the Peloponnesian War to become the leading city of all Greece.

silhouette: The dark shape and outline of someone or something against a brighter or lighter background.

Surrealism: A 20th-century avant-garde movement that began in the 1920s. Surrealist writers and artists (including Salvador Dalí, 1904–1989, and René Magritte, 1898–1967) experimented with contrasting images together in an artwork, often in a surprising or unexpected way. They were also fascinated with dreams and the mysteries of the subconscious. Surrealism was launched in Paris in 1924 by French poet André Breton (1896–1966) with the publication of his *Surrealist Manifesto*. Surrealism became an international movement, widely influencing art, literature, and the cinema as well as social attitudes and behavior.

Symbolism: An artistic and poetic movement or style using symbolic images to express ideas, emotions, or states of mind. It originated in late 19th-century France and Belgium. Its most important figures included the poet Stéphane Mallarmé (1842–1898) and the artist Odilon Redon (1840–1916).

Tools of the trade

To make the most out of the activities in this book, some pointers regarding preparation and supplies are listed below:

- All of the art supplies listed in the activities should be easily obtainable from grocery stores, art and hobby shops, and hardware outlets. However, if you are having difficulty sourcing anything, the Internet has a wealth of retailers that can deliver supplies directly to your house.

- It is advisable to cover the area in which you are working with a waterproof sheet before you start any art activity. Remember to wash your tools and clean up your work area after the activity is over.

- It is a good idea to cover up in an old T-shirt or apron before activities get messy.

- If you can, try to use good-quality materials (such as brushes and paints) over poor-quality ones; you'll notice that it makes a big difference to the result of your art project, and good-quality materials are usually easier to work with.

- When buying brushes for any of the painting projects featured in the book, please note that brushes are numbered according to size: the smaller the number, the finer the brush.

- For media like watercolors, use two bowls of water to rinse your brushes so that the next color you use is not affected by the previous one.

- School glue is used throughout this book, because it is water soluble and dries well. It is available from many suppliers and is sometimes called white glue. A mix of one part water to two parts glue will create a shiny varnish that can be painted over your work to seal it in place.

Index

Picture credits

All works copyright of the artists.